Foreign Investment and Political Conflict in Developing Countries

Foreign Investment and Political Conflict in Developing Countries

John M. Rothgeb, Jr.

Westport, Connecticut
London

Library of Congress Cataloging-in-Publication Data

Rothgeb, John M.
    Foreign investment and political conflict in developing countries
/ John M. Rothgeb, Jr.
        p.   cm.
    Includes bibliographical references and index.
    ISBN 0–275–94548–0 (alk. paper)
    1. Investments, Foreign—Developing countries. 2. International
economic relations. 3. Developing countries—Politics and
government. 4. Political violence—Developing countries.
I. Title.
HG5993.R668   1996
332.6'73'091724—dc20   96–16280

British Library Cataloguing in Publication Data is available.

Library of Congress Catalog Card Number: 96–16280
ISBN: 0–275–94548–0

First published in 1996

Praeger Publishers, 88 Post Road West, Westport, CT 06881
An imprint of Greenwood Publishing Group, Inc.

Printed in the United States of America

The paper used in this book complies with the
Permanent Paper Standard issued by the National
Information Standards Organization (Z39.48–1984).

10   9   8   7   6   5   4   3   2   1

CONTENTS

TABLES

INTERDEPENDENCE AND DOMESTIC CONFLICT

This book is about the political effects of the international dependence of developing countries. The focus is on the degree to which the existence of international economic linkages may be associated with the patterns of political conflict and violence that are found within the world's poorest countries. At least four things point to the need for a careful analysis of these relationships. The first is the often-found tendency for the internal conflicts of developing countries to spread both to engulf neighbors and to incite broader international disputes. The second centers on the international economic disruptions produced by conflict in developing countries. The third relates to the domestic social and economic costs of conflicts in underdeveloped countries and to the roadblocks that these conflicts create that obstruct the path to progress. The fourth has to do with the frequency with which a deeper involvement in the world's commercial networks on the part of developing countries is treated as the best approach to overcoming their poverty.

The relationship between political conflict in developing countries and international instability has long been recognized. Throughout the Cold War, in their attempts to gain advantages over one another, the United States and the Soviet Union frequently intervened in the domestic disputes of developing countries. For instance, one might point to the American involvements in what were initially domestic disputes in Vietnam, Cuba, the Dominican Republic, Grenada, and Nicaragua. In addition to supplying the anti-American forces in several of the conflicts just mentioned, the Soviets intervened in such places as Angola, Ethiopia, and Somalia. The Cold War years brought other examples of how problems in developing countries can lead to broader international crises. Among others, there were the Belgian and United Nations interventions in the Congo in the early 1960s, the Indian role in the war in Pakistan in 1971, the Cuban participation in the Angolan Civil War, the Israeli and Syrian interventions in Lebanon, and the French and Libyan involvement in Chad. Between 1945 and 1988 there were sixty civil wars in developing countries. In seventeen cases, or 28 percent of the time, these civil wars were judged such a serious threat to the interests of other countries that the other countries intervened, thereby substantially widening an already serious problem.[1]

The end of the Cold War has done little to solve the problems associated with the tendency for developing country conflicts to spread. Recent years have witnessed the death by assassination of an Indian prime minister who sought to mediate the Tamil-Sinhalese violence in Sri Lanka, American and United Nations efforts in a Somalia that is torn by civil war, international attempts to quell the anti-democratic elements in Haiti, and an ongoing foreign intervention in the Iraqi government's attempts to suppress its Kurdish population. It is generally agreed that domestic disputes in developing countries now constitute one of the severest threats to international order. One of the most important tasks confronting those who wish to promote a more peaceful world centers on understanding and preventing conflict in the world's poorest countries.

Developing country conflicts also disrupt international commercial networks, producing unemployment, inflation, and wrecked development plans. The extreme international dislocations that accompanied the Iranian Revolution in 1979 serve as an example, for the diminished flow of petroleum that resulted as Iran was torn by domestic discord contributed greatly to double digit inflation and unemployment among advanced industrialized countries and to extreme misery in those developing countries that imported oil. One can expect the potential for such international disturbances to multiply in coming years as the world becomes more reliant on the resources and markets found in the developing world. Again, studying the reasons for conflict in poverty-stricken societies is essential for those interested in a more stable international system.

A third reason for studying political conflict in the developing world is the effect it has on development. Substantial human costs are always incurred when conflict and violence break out in very poor societies. Civil wars in Ethiopia, Sudan, and Somalia have resulted in widespread famines that have killed many thousands of people. In Uganda, the civil violence of the 1980s so disrupted the economy that per capita income fell from $949 in 1980, one of the highest figures in sub-Saharan Africa, to $31 in 1985, one of the lowest levels.[2] The social costs of domestic conflict multiply as one scans the developing world, with terrorism and guerrilla warfare in Peru, Colombia, and the Philippines blocking economic development, violence in Sri Lanka costing that country its once highly profitable tourist trade, and riots and labor unrest in Haiti and Panama sapping the ability to promote a sustained program of growth and development. Political conflict and violence in the developing world constitutes such a source of misery and wasted resources that there is little doubt that it will prove impossible to promote much progress in the afflicted societies until such disputes are brought under control.[3]

These considerations have led to considerable research that is devoted to exploring the origins of political conflict and violence. Snyder (1978), Zimmermann (1983), and Lichbach (1989) provide excellent reviews of much of this research literature. One feature of this body of work that is of special concern to the present effort is the general absence of systematic efforts to explore the manner in which a society's international dependence may affect its patterns of domestic conflict. Zimmermann (1983, 204–205) notes that external linkages "have only begun to gain close attention as predictors of [domestic] political violence and instability," and London and Robinson (1989, 307) state, "It is imperative that . . . international causal factors be examined in future studies focusing on collective political violence." Skocpol (1979, 20) agrees, maintaining that while they have been understudied, international forces are an integral part of the process by which domestic social and political grievances are translated into domestic conflict and violence. Snyder (1978, 501), Goldstone (1980, 448), Stohl (1980, 325), and Gurr and Lichbach (1986, 32) concur, stating that there is a need for research to determine whether international dependence produces conflict, what type, under what conditions, and for how long.

Investigating the relationship between the international dependence and domestic political conflict of developing countries is particularly important in light of the many internationally oriented development schemes that have been proposed over the last four decades. In the early 1960s, the Alliance for Progress and the Peace Corps were launched as liberal American plans for eliminating the misery of underdevelopment that supposedly bred communism. The 1970s brought radical proposals for a New International Economic Order that would closely tie developing countries to a reformed international order operating on principles that were designed to provide guaranteed markets and income. In the 1980s, more conservative free-market ideas were put forward, with the Caribbean Basin Initiative, which envisioned tackling underdevelopment by giving businesses incentives to locate in developing countries, serving as a leading example. Today, one finds the creation of free trade agreements, such as the North American Free Trade Agreement (NAFTA), touted as the best way to solve the problems confronting some poor countries.

In each case, one can discern a common element in the strategy pursued: The belief that closer international economic ties of one sort or another can make a fundamental contribution to overcoming the challenges of poverty and the notion that the benefits of such linkages will far outweigh the social and political costs that developing countries might be required to pay for establishing those linkages. The faith in these approaches to development is often so great that it is assumed that it is obvious that benefits will far exceed costs, and one rarely finds any recognition of the possibility that they may lead to political and social problems. One of the central contentions of this book is that this assumption may be wrong. As one scholar writes, "It looks increasingly as though the [international] effort to achieve growth, whether or not successful, brings with it calamitous side effects in the political realm" (Hirschman 1979, 61–62). It is essential to subject the relationship between international dependence and domestic political conflict to careful empirical scrutiny, for the failure to do so may inflict unnecessary suffering on those who must bear the burdens associated with development strategies that are built on promoting international dependence and interdependence.[4]

Reinforcing these concerns is the substantial consensus in the international political economy literature that international dependence strongly affects developing societies. Holsti (1975, 833), Krasner (1976, 319), Gasiorowski (1985, 341), and Clark (1989, 173) explain that the smaller resource bases of poorer countries render them more susceptible to dominance by others and to the vicissitudes of international markets, creating a greater probablity of unfortunate social outcomes. Haggard (1990, 3) argues that among developing countries, "international shocks and pressures, and the domestic . . . crises associated with them, have been the most powerful stimuli for change."

When taken together, these considerations point to the need for systematic work that is directed toward the analysis of why domestic discord occurs in developing societies and how the international dependence of those countries might contribute to the onset and exacerbation of that conflict. In conducting such research, one must first specify and define the concepts that serve as the focal points for the investigation. The next section does this by considering briefly the definitions of international dependence and interdependence and of domestic conflict.

DEFINING INTERDEPENDENCE AND CONFLICT

Interdependence

Within the context of this book, interdependence is defined as a situation in which two or more international actors have a mutual need for one another that is based on an exchange of goods and services.[5] Such exchanges are generally conceptualized in commercial and economic terms, with such things as international trade, foreign investments, international credit transactions, and foreign aid receiving the most attention as possible sources of interdependence. The basic idea behind the examination of such forces centers on the notion that, in any transaction, one has a provider (an exporter, an investor, a lender, or a dispenser of aid) and a customer, both of whom benefit from the relationship. The provider secures such things as markets, profits, dividends, and so forth, while the customer obtains access to goods or services that it needs or wants. Neither can produce for itself or only can produce at a prohibitively high cost.[6]

Within an interdependent relationship, dependence refers to the degree to which one partner needs the other(s). Dependence is used when discussing one part of the more complex interdependent association. While the term interdependence pertains to the overall situation that exists when actors engage in the exchange of goods and services, dependence focuses on how the relationship affects one of the actors within that relationship, with the concern usually centering on how a particular actor finds that its international transactions restrict it in some way.[7] To the extent that one partner in a relationship is considered more entangled than the others, the overall relationship is usually labelled a case of asymmetrical interdependence (Dolan et al. 1982; Dolan and Tomlin 1984). The discussion of dependence centers on the degree to which an asymmetrical relationship robs an actor of its autonomy and the ability to make its own policy selections and has other deleterious consequences, such as slower economic growth, fewer jobs, and political controversy, for the society experiencing the dependence (Caporaso 1978, 18).

Several types of commercial ties can serve as the basis for an interdependent relationship, including trade in goods and services, international loans, and foreign investments. Many analysts see the linkages resulting from direct foreign investments as among the most potent of the international forces that contribute to the creation of interdependence. Direct foreign investments are defined as property within a society that is owned by non-nationals, with the foreigners retaining managerial control of their assets. By contrast, portfolio investments include property that non-nationals own but over which they do not retain managerial control.[8]

As Rothgeb (1989b, 4–6) notes, in recent years the dependence stemming from direct foreign investments has been a source of extreme controversy. One reason is the immense volume of financial resources that increasingly flow across the world's borders (Freiden 1991, 428). Another is that these investments often are perceived as giving foreigners control over the most dynamic sectors of the local economy. A third is that the bulk of such investments are made by multinational corporations with ties of national origin to advanced industrial home countries. Multinational corporations consist of a cluster of businesses joined together by bonds of common ownership that are able to exploit a common pool of resources and that operate according to a common strategy. These corporations have headquarters in one country, known as the home country, and subsidiaries in other countries, known as host states (Vernon 1971, 4–11).

Much of the debate about multinational corporations stems from the vast economic resources, technological secrets, and entrepreneurial talent that they control. Surveys comparing the total sales of the world's largest firms with the total gross domestic products of the countries (large and small, developed and developing) found around the globe routinely reveal that many of the largest international economic actors are multinational corporations, which often have substantially more potential economic clout than many countries (Rothgeb 1989b; Billet 1991). These capabilities create for multinational firms the image of a behemoth that is able to dominate not only smaller, purely domestic business competitors but also governments, particularly those governing the poor societies located in the developing world.

The upshot is a situation in which the direct foreign investments found within a nation are regarded as possibly having a strong influence on its political climate and on the degree to which it experiences political conflict. As seen in later chapters, while there are many conceptions and much argument about exactly how foreign investments affect a host state's pattern of political conflict, few systematic studies have attempted to assess the empirical validity of these contentions. Given the extensive role that many international development plans reserve for direct foreign investment, it is imperative that scholars develop a better appreciation for how this form of dependence is related to conflict. This book is designed as a step in that direction.

Domestic Conflict

As far as conflict is concerned, domestic discord comes in many forms, including criminal activities such as murder and robbery, organized political strikes and protests, the large-scale group acts of violence that occur during riots, and the extremely deadly behavior associated with terrorism, guerrilla warfare, and civil wars. While all forms of conflict and violence are important subjects of study, the concern in this book is with the analysis of political conflict, which is defined as overt public action by nongovernmental actors that protests government policy and that is designed to induce a change either in the policy or in the composition of the government. This form of conflict is examined because it directly threatens the viability of a society, has the potential for undermining and destroying a government, and is far more likely than forms of conflict such as crime to lead to attempts at foreign intervention.

While the relationship between interdependence and domestic political conflict has not received much attention in previous systematic analysis, there have been a number of studies designed to explore the degree to which one can discern different forms of political conflict. For instance, research by Rummel (1966, 61–67), Tanter (1966, 49), and Hibbs (1973, 9) indicates that domestic conflict is multidimensional, including analytically and empirically distinct elements that they label as political turmoil and internal war. Turmoil is defined as a relatively spontaneous form of violent conflict that usually is carried out against property and that is touched off by particularly unpopular government decisions. Examples would be the riots found in the 1980s in Egypt and Venezuela when those governments announced plans to modify government subsidies designed to help the poor purchase basic necessities. Internal war is a highly organized and violent form of conflict directed at the members and supporters of a government for the purpose of toppling the government or inducing it to change policies to which it is dedicated. Examples of this form of violence include the terrorism and guerrilla warfare conducted by the Tamils in their attempt to secede from Sri Lanka and the guerrilla war found in El Salvador throughout much of the 1970s and 1980s.

Gurr and Lichbach (1986, 5–6, 34) build on these distinctions, arguing that it is important that researchers distinguish between protest, which involves conflict about the content of government policies, and rebellion, which centers on attempts to overthrow the government violently. These authors also note the value of differentiating between violent and nonviolent protests, with the violent form tending toward spontaneity and the nonviolent form usually displaying a high degree of organizational activity. When combined with the above categories of conflict, one finds similarities between what Rummel, Tanter, and Hibbs label as turmoil and Gurr and Lichbach refer to as violent protest, and between what the former call internal war and the latter call rebellion, leaving an additional form, herein referred to as protest, of highly organized nonviolent conflict that is designed to change government policy.

Past empirical research indicates that domestic political conflict has three basic dimensions that one may label protest, turmoil, and internal war.[9] Each of these aspects of conflict are examined to determine how they are affected by the dependence resulting from direct foreign investments. In doing so, this book contributes to a better understanding of why differing types of domestic conflict occur and how international forces are involved in the process.[10]

ORGANIZATION OF THE BOOK

In spite of the potential importance of examining the relationship between dependence and domestic political conflict in developing countries, empirical research on the subject has been relatively scarce. While there has been a dearth of systematic analysis, a perusal of the international political economy literature reveals a substantial body of speculative and polemical work. In general, one can discern three basic types of scholarly arguments regarding the manner in which dependence is hypothesized as affecting domestic political conflict.[11] The first is based on the premise that dependence affects conflict by way of a prior impact on the patterns of scarcity and deprivation found in the host society. The second sees dependence as creating conflict by altering the basic competitive relationships among key actors in society. The third treats dependence as a spur to antiforeign nationalist conflict and violence. These arguments serve to organize this book.

In Chapter 2, the relationship between foreign investment, deprivation, and conflict is considered. The discussion begins with a brief examination of deprivation-based conceptions of why domestic conflict occurs and how foreign investments are hypothesized as contributing to the process. Many international theorists see foreign investments as creating hardships in developing societies by encouraging intolerable disparities between the incomes of the rich and the poor, by stunting economic growth and development, by enticing governments to use repressive tactics to excess, and by accumulating large agricultural holdings that dispossess peasants, leaving them homeless and unemployed. These processes and the various schools of thought that surround them in the international political economy literature are examined, and a systematic research design is set up and employed to assess the degree to which they are supported by cross-national evidence.

In Chapter 3, the focus shifts to the examination of how foreign investments might create conflict by changing the relative positions of differing elements in society. These changes are expected to occur because international contacts mean that some groups benefit while others face new challenges. Benefits supposedly flow to those parts of society that are efficient and thereby profit by supplying and interacting with the foreigners, while problems arise for those that are inefficient because the foreign presence means additional competition. In either case, the projected result is political conflict as the winners and losers in this process act either to demand new political influence or to prevent the erosion of their political bases. As is the case in Chapter 2, a cross-national research design is used to explore these possibilities.

Chapter 4 investigates the degree to which the social forces at work within a developing country may produce a nationalistic reaction against foreign investments. The following are at least three types of processes that may create such a backlash: (1) the rapid change associated with the urbanization and industrialization that may coincide with a foreign presence; (2) the fear of neo-imperialism; and (3) the possibility that foreigners may be perceived as favoring one domestic ethnic or national faction over others. The cross-national research design employed in Chapters 2 and 3 will be used to explore each of these possibilities systematically.

Chapter 5 summarizes the basic points made in the previous chapters. Also, this chapter discusses the implications of the empirical results for resolving conflict and encouraging development in the Third World.

NOTES

1. See Rothgeb (1993a, 76). It should be noted that a civil war is defined as a situation in which organized armed violence occurs between a recognized government and some portion of its domestic opposition. Data relating to civil wars since 1945 may be found in Singer 1991.

2. These figures are from the United Nations, *Yearbook of National Accounts Statistics*, 1985.

3. Olson (1982, 4) notes the widespread agreement among economists that a stable political environment is an essential part of the social climate that must exist in order to promote economic growth and development.

4. In his discussion of the Alliance for Progress, Wiarda (1986–1987, 141) echoes these sentiments by noting the degree to which internationally oriented development schemes may become a source of considerable political instability by unleashing social and political forces that governments are not prepared to handle.

5. Caporaso (1978) provides one of the earliest and best discussions of how to conceptualize and define dependence and interdependence.

6. Although interdependence usually is seen in commercial and economic terms, it should be noted that political, military, and ideological resources might serve as the basis for the transactions that create interdependence. As an example, one might consider the recently terminated American relationship with the Philippines wherein the United States gained access to Philippine territory for air and naval bases in exchange for cash payments and protection during the Cold War.

7. As it is used in the international literature, dependence almost always has at least a slightly (and sometimes a pronounced) negative connotation, focusing on how an actor's external relations restrict it in some way. At least at a conceptual level, however, it is possible to see dependence in positive terms, for external relations may have a liberating effect when they allow an actor access to goods that it cannot produce for itself or allow an actor to use its resources more efficiently.

8. For a classic definition of foreign investment and of the role multinational corporations play in the investment process, see Vernon 1971. A discussion of the controversy surrounding foreign investment and multinational corporate activities in developing countries is found in Vernon 1976, 1977 and in Rothgeb 1986a, 1987, 1989b.

9. One important point should be noted regarding these different types of conflict: They are both conceptually and empirically distinct from one another. Previous empirical research indicates both that the various forms of behavior that serve as measures for these types of conflict form empirically separate dimensions when factor analyzed (Rummel 1966; Tanter 1966) and that different types of social forces appear to produce each of these forms of conflict (Hibbs 1973; Gurr and Lichbach 1986).

10. Snyder (1978), Skocpol (1979), and Goldstone (1980) state that there is a need for greater precision in the study of domestic conflict and violence and argue for an analytical approach that focuses on several types of conflict and investigates a variety of possible mechanisms that may lead to conflict.

11. These arguments are organized according to categories that several scholars regard as appropriate. For example, Snyder (1978), Muller (1985b), and Lichbach (1989) discuss two fundamental approaches to the study of conflict, one focusing on deprivation and the other on the competitive relationships among key actors in society, which they label as the deprivation and mobilization approaches, respectively. Feierabend and Feierabend (1966) describe a third, referred to as displacement, that is similar to the nationalist approach.

CHAPTER 2

FOREIGN INVESTMENT, DEPRIVATION, AND CONFLICT

This chapter investigates systematically the degree to which the penetration of developing countries by multinational corporations leads to increased levels of domestic political conflict because it creates a degree of deprivation that at least some members of the local population find intolerable. The discussion in this chapter is divided into three sections. The first describes four basic mechanisms by which foreign investments supposedly lead to deprivation and examines the controversy in the international political economy literature that surrounds the question of whether foreign investments actually contribute to any of the processes under consideration. The second presents the cross-national research design that is employed to test the arguments found in the first section. Finally, the results are presented and analyzed in an attempt to determine the degree to which they support any of the points of view found in the scholarly literature.

DEPRIVATION AND CONFLICT

The contention that some form of deprivation is the basic cause of social and political conflict is arguably the oldest explanation found in the social science literature.[1] The fundamental thrust of the deprivation thesis centers on the relatively simple idea that people are prone toward some sort of action when they confront social circumstances that they consider unacceptably harsh and foreboding and that they believe they should not have to tolerate. Under such conditions, a feeling of frustration builds that eventually is released as aggression toward those that are held responsible for such a state of affairs. Deprivation arguments are built on a foundation that assumes the following: (1) that bad social conditions will create a feeling of frustration and anger among the people that experience them, (2) that those who are angry and frustrated are able to identify a target that is responsible for the bad conditions, and (3) that the anger and frustration that is experienced will lead to a particular form of aggression—conflict.[2]

Often, the aggression stemming from social frustration will be of a nonpolitical nature and may not even be violent, for the target held accountable for the trouble at hand will not be a government figure and the aggressive response will fall within the range of acceptable social behavior. However, when the provocation is especially extreme and when it appears as a part of a general pattern of governmental behavior, political action may be at hand. As Locke (1955, 187–188) wrote:

When the people are made miserable, and find themselves exposed to the ill-usage of arbitrary power . . . if a long train of [government] abuses, prevarications and artifices, all tending in the same way, make the design visible to the people . . . it is not to be wondered that they should rouse themselves and endeavor to put the rule into such hands which may secure to them the ends for which government was at first erected.

While Locke focused on how government behavior might lead to aggression based on frustration, others have concentrated on the process by which people become inclined toward conflict. At least two approaches can be used for studying the latter question. The first is psychological and pays close attention to how individuals respond to negative stimuli. The second is societal, with the investigation examining the specific types of conditions found in a community that are associated with greater levels of conflict.[3] Employing the latter approach, Gurr (1968, 1104) suggests that one must think in comparative terms when studying the severity of the social factors that lead to conflict:

The basic theoretical proposition is that . . . deprivation is the basic precondition for civil strife of any kind, and that the more widespread and intense deprivation is among members of a population, the greater is the magnitude of strife in one or another form . . . deprivation is defined as actors' perceptions of discrepancy between their value expectations (the goods and conditions of life to which they believe they are justifiably entitled) and their value capabilities (the amounts of those goods and conditions that they think they are able to get and keep).

In other words, according to Gurr, Locke's view is incomplete, for conflict is not simply a product of the frustration that results from not having what one wants or needs. Instead, people are inclined toward conflict when they think that society should be providing them with more than it does, when the gap between what they expect and what they receive is especially large, and (by extension) when the current governmental and social frameworks are held responsible for these gaps.[4] Trouble brews on such occasions because these are the conditions that lead people to question the legitimacy of those who rule, with the key to legitimacy residing in large part in the ability of the system to maintain a tolerable gap between a people's expectations and what is actually delivered.[5]

Among the most important challenges for deprivation theorists are those revolving around determining, first, the sorts of social and political circumstances that lead people to perceive such an unacceptable gap between their value expectations and value capabilities that they engage in antigovernment political behavior and, second, the types of action that might result. A careful examination of the literature on political conflict reveals that scholars have focused on four basic types of forces responsible for pushing people toward deprivation-based conflict. The first might be referred to as involving absolute deprivation, the second as relative deprivation, the third as agrarian or land-based deprivation, and the fourth as political deprivation.[6]

Absolute Deprivation

Arguments built on the notion that absolute deprivation is the source of domestic political conflict rest on the belief that people are prepared only to accept a given level of misery and no more. There is a threshold of poverty and suffering that people can tolerate and when they are pushed below that threshold, they will turn to conflict in an effort either to escape from their suffering or to strike out at those that they regard as responsible for their plight. These arguments are at the heart of Marxist conceptions of political conflict. As Marx and Engels (1959, 19) wrote, "The modern laborer . . . instead of rising with the progress of industry, sinks deeper and deeper . . . he becomes a pauper . . . and here it becomes evident that the bourgeoisie is unfit any longer to be the ruling class of society."[7] In its most basic form, the absolute deprivation argument asserts that there is a great deal of potential volatility among people who suffer from extreme poverty, for such individuals have few possessions and as a result have little to lose by challenging the government through political conflict.

The notion that extreme poverty propels people toward conflict has been the subject of considerable controversy. A century and a half ago, Alexis de Tocqueville (1971) rejected the idea that the poor are most prone toward conflict when he commented that in the years before the French Revolution, the poorest parts of France were not the primary centers of political disruption, noting that "it is a singular fact that . . . steadily increasing prosperity, far from tranquilizing the population, everywhere promoted a spirit of unrest," and that "it was precisely in those parts of France where there had been most improvement that popular discontent ran highest." Brinton (1965, 250) reached the same basic conclusion in his classic study of revolutions, stating that political violence seems "to originate in the discontents of not unprosperous people who feel restraint, cramp, annoyance, rather than downright crushing oppression." Moore (1966, 101) concurs that "severe suffering does not always and necessarily generate revolutionary outbursts."

In recent years, scholars have devoted renewed attention to absolute deprivation, arguing that poverty in itself is not the source of conflict. Instead, trouble is seen as a product of the interaction between poverty and some sort of change for the worse in the social circumstances that confront the poor, such as a decline in per capita growth. People are not described as taking part in political conflict simply because they are miserable. Boswell and Dixon (1993, 685) contend that "even highly exploited workers and peasants are unlikely to rebel if economic growth promises to improve their lives." The probability of conflict increases most rapidly when poverty is combined with changes that push people beyond the threshold mentioned. Tanter and Midlarsky (1967, 270) see economic declines, rather than absolute misery, as the source of conflict. Gerschwender (1968, 133) observes that "[unfavorable] changes in objective conditions produce a state of mind in which individuals believe that they are unjustly deprived of a better way of life." An economic crisis makes the poor "vulnerable to the whip of increased exploitation and the specter of unemployment" because "the lack of growth renders [the] distribution [of resources] more zero-sum" (Boswell and Dixon 1993, 685).

A downturn in the economy is regarded as creating the seeds for conflict by producing still more misery piled on top of what was already a barely tolerable situation, leading to the comparison (across time) between value expectations (which may remain relatively constant) and the society's value capabilities (which were very low to begin with and are now declining quickly) that Gurr hypothesized as a key to the conflict process. Examples of conflict resulting from this sort of a process are found in the urban riots that occurred in Egypt, Tunisia, and Venezuela in the 1980s. Extremely poverty-stricken segments of the population found themselves facing the additional plagues of collapsing growth in per capita income, growing unemployment, inflation, and cuts in government budgets leading to decreased price supports for foodstuffs and other basic goods.

Relative Deprivation

Conflict resulting from relative deprivation is found when the distribution of resources and incomes in a society is so unequal that the have-nots feel compelled to take action in an attempt to secure a greater share for themselves. For centuries, political thinkers have regarded inequality as a potent source of trouble. In ancient Greece, Aristotle (1971, 87) stated that "when inferior, people enter on strife in order that they may be equal." Madison (1961, 79) wrote in the same vein in Federalist #10, contending that "the most common and durable source of [conflict among] factions has been the various and unequal distribution of property." Recently, Kornhauser (1959, 151) has argued that "highly visible differentials in economic gains [lead to] strong feelings of alienation from the existing order . . . among those in the rapidly developing sectors and areas," and Sigelman and Simpson (1977, 106) note that "according to [a] diverse literature, anti-system frustrations are apt to be high where a substantial portion of the public does not share fully in the allocation of scarce resources." Muller and Seligson (1987, 427) agree that an "important direct cause of . . . political violence . . . is inequality in the distribution of income."

Lichbach (1989, 432) observes that many class-based conceptions of social conflict, which have been extremely popular among both academics and would-be leaders of social movements, are based on some type of relative deprivation. The fundamental thrust of these arguments is that people are driven to conflict not because they have been forced into an existence in which they barely receive enough income to meet their basic needs, but that they enter into strife because they resent deeply the fact that some members of society have accumulated property and are compensated at levels that greatly exceed their own. In other words, people are regarded as constantly comparing what they have to what others have and become so upset that they are prepared to resort to conflict when they see large disparities. Of course, this assumes that people are aware of and pay close attention to the distribution of resources within their society, that there is no widely accepted value structure that justifies an unequal distribution of resources, and that people will conclude that political conflict (rather than working harder or changing jobs to get higher pay) is the appropriate response to such inequities (Weede 1981, 640–641; Lichbach 1989, 456–457).

Many analysts maintain that inequality is a particularly potent source of trouble in developing countries. Two reasons are offered. The first is the widespread poverty in such societies, which is said to intensify the resentment that the less privileged feel when comparing their lot to that of those who are well-off. According to Midlarsky (1988, 492), the probability of political trouble is highest when there is an elite that enjoys immense benefits while most people experience misery, referring to the "difference principle" when describing these conditions. In this line of thought, poverty and inequality interact. In itself, poverty is not a problem as long as there is little inequality because everyone is in the same boat and there is no target for conflict. At the same time, inequality is no cause for concern where the standard of living for most people is high (as in advanced industrialized countries) because there will be less inclination to resent differences in resource distribution since they will not mean the difference between extremely marginal and opulent ways of life.[8]

A second factor that makes developing countries susceptible to conflict based on relative deprivation is their tendency toward promoting rapid development. Speedy economic growth frequently leads to distortions in the distribution of income as some members of society benefit from the change sooner than others (Olson 1963). Also, Cardoso (1979, 43) and O'Donnell (1988, 31–32) argue that in their attempts to achieve fast growth, developing country governments may promote policies that encourage disparities in the distribution of resources in the belief that accumulating and mobilizing the vast resources needed for industrialization requires a concentration of income in the hands of a favored few. In either case, the end product is political and social unrest as those who are left behind become upset when they compare their suffering to the lives of those who are better off. The political conflict and violence found in Argentina, Brazil, Chile, and Iran in the 1970s are examples of these types of circumstances.[9]

Agrarian Deprivation

In most developing countries, the agricultural sector plays an important role as a vital source of goods and services, jobs, and as the bedrock upon which many people's lives are organized. As a result, disruptions and untoward occurrences in this arena are often treated by scholars as a key to political conflict (Huntington 1968; Migdal 1974; Paige 1975; Skocpol 1982; Midlarsky 1982; Midlarsky and Roberts 1985; Mason 1986; Prosterman and Riedinger 1987; Anderson 1990; Brockett 1991). The basic thrust of much of this literature is that when change comes to the agricultural sector the result is usually unemployed peasants who have few prospects for finding an alternative way of life. Given the hand-to-mouth style of existence for many peasants, unemployment spells an economic crisis of enormous proportions, for it means that an already meager way of life now will become nearly unendurable, which may lead to increased political conflict.

In general, the force that sets off this process is usually seen as a growing commercialization of the agricultural sector. Commercialization involves a process wherein agricultural interests abandon strict subsistence farming and begin to produce for more than local markets. Commercialization is seen as creating new patterns of ownership and employment, both of which displace peasants, leaving them without the incomes and social services that they are accustomed to. As Mason (1986, 492) says, "Among the processes of change that are most corrosive to the legitimacy and stability of the [agricultural sector is] commercialization." Brockett (1991, 255) agrees, noting that "peasant mobilization [for political conflict] usually originated in areas where the conversion of land to the production of commercial export crops promoted the expulsion of subsistence peasants." Moore (1966) and Migdal (1974) concur.

As peasants are forced away from their occupations, they experience greater poverty as already meager incomes dry up. At the same time, they also are marginalized, for they lose their traditional roles in society and are set adrift with no sense of exactly where they fit into the new world beyond their villages. They confront a new social universe that is entirely alien to the way of life they have always known (Kornhauser 1959, 145; Migdal 1974, 173). As Holsti (1982, 11) observes, "To many among these people, integration and interdependence [with the commercial world] imply cultural dilution and possibly extinction." According to Anderson's findings (1990, 100), the increased poverty and sense of injustice that are created by these circumstances are the sorts of conditions that push peasants toward more extreme forms of political conflict. Prosterman and Riedinger (1987, 10–11) and Brockett (1992, 172) also agree that the sweeping changes and the landlessness that accompany the processes just described are a potent source of trouble.[10]

The changes resulting from the commercialization of the agrarian sector affect the ability of peasants to obtain important social services. Migdal (1974) and Mason (1986) explain that in developing countries many key social and commercial services for the poorest people, such as health care, education, and loans for the purchase of seed, livestock, and equipment, are provided not by the government or by large corporations but are made available by the wealthier members of the rural community. As the agricultural sector is commercialized, ownership patterns become more concentrated as large businesses from outside the rural community acquire land for the purpose of selling to new and more profitable markets. When this happens, the availability of social services changes because some of the former providers may sell out and leave the community while others may decide to change the terms of the arrangements they formerly offered to those who needed the services. Whichever happens, the provision of services dries up or becomes more expensive. When former providers leave, the supply of services contracts and the price increases. And changes in the terms for offering services will reflect the relative bargaining abilities of providers and purchasers, with purchasers suffering from the disadvantages of having few choices and uncertain incomes (if any) as job availability is restricted by the circumstances described.

Whether the deprivation results from the loss of jobs or from the absence of essential services that disappear as outsiders move in, the result is the same: The probability of conflict and violence goes up as peasants feel that they have no other option if they are to avoid outright ruin. The stormy political conditions found in parts of Central America and in Peru in the 1970s and 1980s are often described as examples of these processes.

Political Deprivation

Political deprivation is said to exist when a government acts to deny the people certain types of social services that normally are expected from the government, to impose new demands on the people that are perceived as unreasonable or unfair, or to restrict or punish attempts to criticize the government or air grievances. Many analysts argue that the best and most accurate explanations for political conflict are found not in the sorts of economic conditions described but reside in the relationship between the people and their government. As Moore (1966, 454) writes, "The evidence is clearly negative . . . that . . . a decline in the [people's] material situation [and] a massive threat to their way of life . . . bring about a revolutionary situation."

Instead, the most important determinant of uprisings and outbursts supposedly is lodged in how the government relates to the people. When a population is treated in a benign and understanding manner and when they are given ample opportunity to express their grievances through normal and nonviolent political channels, it is maintained that there will be little inclination toward trouble, even if economic conditions are unfavorable (Moore 1966, 34; Muller 1985b, 48; Muller and Seligson 1987, 429). In such circumstances, most members of society will even countenance a government's use of force to suppress those who turn to violence, for the use of such tactics by opponents of the government will be viewed as beyond the realm of accepted behavior. As Johnson (1966, 92) argues, "Well-socialized actors will continue to expect authorities to control deviancy during times of change."

According to this line of thought, the greatest problems come when a government is unresponsive, refuses to provide the people with access to the means for expressing grievances, and seeks to suppress and punish those who are critical and exclude them from the normal avenues of political participation. When this happens, the likelihood of conflict greatly increases, for when "the state is geared to the maintenance of powerlessness among excluded groups, these groups have little choice other than insurgency" or some other form of conflict (Griffin 1992, 130). Chazan (1982, 181) and Aya (1984, 328) suggest that repression rarely accomplishes its central purpose of dampening conflict and that its actual effect is to force those with deep-seated grievances to change tactics, gearing their efforts toward forms of protest and conflict that either are less risky or that are directed from beyond the government's reach, such as, from exile or from remote parts of the country that are difficult to reach. This has been the case with many guerrilla and terrorist organizations. Repression merely transforms, but does little to eliminate, conflict.

Another line of thought is found in the literature that depicts the relationship between repression and conflict as curvilinear. According to this view, both very low and very high levels of repression are associated with a smaller incidence of conflict. When repression is extremely severe and well organized, people become fearful of the consequences of participation, have difficulties cooperating with one another for the purpose of engaging in conflict, and find that acts that are launched are ephemeral because they are quickly squelched (Muller 1985b, 48; Muller and Seligson 1987, 429; Mainwaring 1987, 144). At intermediate levels of repression, however, conflict is more likely because, on the one hand, avenues for peacefully presenting grievances are not readily available, while on the other hand, the government's behavior is such as to create discontent at its restrictions on the people and at its arbitrary and unjust actions. When repression is used only intermittently, people may come to believe that they can act with impunity and without risk because of the chance that their particular act of conflict will go unpunished. As Muller and Seligson (1987, 430) put it:

Because opportunities for genuine participation are restricted, many politically activated citizens may come to perceive civil disobedience and violence as being more efficacious than legal means of pseudo-participation; and since the expected costs of insurgency may not be perceived to be prohibitive, rational actors may well attach a relatively high utility to aggressive political behavior.

As was the case with each of the other forms of deprivation, many scholars hypothesize that developing countries are especially susceptible to repression-based conflict. Two arguments are offered to justify this observation. The first focuses on the rapid social change that may be found in developing societies, most notably those that have been opened to foreign influences. Under such circumstances, governments often respond with repressive acts that are designed to allow them to keep a grip on the rate of change (Hibbs 1973, 187). Iran under the Shah is offered as an example (Rubin 1981; Sick 1985; Muller and Seligson 1987, 430). The second argument centers on the attempts of governments in developing countries to promote growth through massive capital accumulation and to treat those who disagree with or question such policies as unpatriotic and deserving of rough treatment, as happened in Argentina, Brazil, and Chile in the 1970s (Cardoso 1979; Hirschman 1979; Kaufman 1979; O'Donnell 1988). Whatever the reason for repression, the end product is projected as increased conflict.

Summary

Deprivation-based arguments are built on the premise that when the political, economic, and social conditions within a community are bad enough the probability of political trouble increases substantially. In considering the case for such arguments, at least four questions must be addressed. The first pertains to the types of discontent that can lead to conflict. A careful analysis of deprivation explanations of instability requires that one isolate and examine specific types of social dislocation. Four are presented. The first, referred to as absolute deprivation, sees conflict as a product of a mix between extreme poverty and a stagnation in the rate of growth in per capita income. The second, labelled relative deprivation, depicts instability as resulting from the interaction between poverty and inequalities in the distribution of incomes. A third views political trouble as derived from problems in the agricultural sector, with the displacement of peseants due to commercialization leading to the dissatisfaction that breeds conflict. Finally, a government's use of repression is described by many scholars as breaking channels for voicing grievances in an orderly way while at the same time creating the sort of deep resentment that ends in violence.

The second issue has to do with the type of society that is most likely to experience the political difficulties stemming from deprivation. For the most part, each of the mechanisms is discussed as most relevant for developing countries and far less applicable to advanced industrialized states. One reason for this has to do with the deep and widespread poverty found in developing societies and the greater affluence of advanced countries, with poverty being a basic ingredient that many believe must be present for deprivation processes to go into effect. A second reason relates to the rapid changes often occurring in developing countries that upset established patterns of social interaction and create the sorts of disturbances that cause people to question their place in society. And finally, developing country governments frequently pursue policies that are designed to promote rapid economic growth at the price of inequality, repression, and economic suffering for the downtrodden.

The third question revolves around the type of conflict that emerges from the four deprivation mechanisms. As the authors of one study point out, the discussion of deprivation usually occurs within the context of attempts to explain why violent social revolutions happen. Such events, however, are rare. Political disturbances of any sort, whether protest, turmoil, or internal war, have sufficient potential for seriously disrupting the often fragile political environment in developing countries that "it is . . . plausible to relax the postulate [relating to] revolution as an inevitable consequence" in order that one might direct one's attention toward the exploration of other forms of domestic conflict and violence (Muller and Seligson 1987, 425). Muller (1985b, 52) astutely observes that, to date, researchers have failed to pin down any specific type of conflict as the only natural outgrowth of deprivation, writing that "the exact nature of the discontent postulated to arise from the macro-economic condition of inequality [and other types of deprivation] is an open question." Clearly, work is needed that focuses on several types of what might be referred to as subrevolutionary political instability.

A final issue relates to the legitimacy of the government. Time and again, one finds deprivation theorists arguing that the miseries produced by one or another type of deprivation only will lead to conflict if those who are deprived come to see the current government and social order as having lost their legitimacy. Johnson (1966) expresses this view when he asserts that "the most important function of the value system in a society is to authorize, or legitimize, the use of force" (26) and "the prime characteristic of revolutionary . . . conditions is the 'loss of authority'" (31). Many authors see this "loss of authority" as a product of external forces (Johnson 1962; Skocpol 1979). As noted in Chapter 1, one of the most powerful external forces in the contemporary international system is the foreign investment of multinational corporations. The next section considers the possible role of such investments in creating the deprivation processes and the decline in legitimacy.

FOREIGN INVESTMENTS AND DEPRIVATION

The relationship between direct foreign investments and the political, social, and economic conditions found in developing countries is one of the most hotly contested and frequently debated topics in the field of international political economy. As noted in Chapter 1, when one combines the size and affluence of many multinational corporations with the weakness, poverty, and desire for rapid economic growth of most developing countries, one has a formula for controversy. Under such circumstances, it probably is only natural that widely divergent opinions will emerge, with some authors arguing that multinational behemoths use their strength to dominate the poor and weak and to destroy those who might get in their way as a part of an overall strategy for securing the greatest profits possible, while others insist that the foreign investments of these multinational giants provide the capital, technology, and entrepreneurial talent that developing countries need in order to grow, prosper, and bring tranquility to what are often troubled societies. A careful review of the literature pertaining to these questions reveals three groups of views regarding the relationship between direct foreign investment and political stability in developing countries.[11] For convenience, these are labelled as the asymmetrical alliance, malevolent influence, and liberal schools of thought.[12]

Asymmetrical Alliance

Those who subscribe to the notion that an asymmetrial alliance exists between foreign firms and host governments in developing countries argue that multinational corporations use their foreign investments in poor societies to achieve a position that allows them to dominate the local scene. Authors holding this view generally operate from the premise that foreign investments are a key element in a contemporary system of imperialism that is designed to allow the world's largest corporations to gain access to inexpensive resources and labor and to siphon capital out of developing countries. Doing this is described as allowing multinational corporations to maintain ever-increasing profit margins by insuring that they will have guaranteed markets where they will face no local competition and low costs of production due to their ability to obtain the cheap raw materials and labor that they need.

Foreign corporations dominate developing countries by purchasing the "commanding heights" of the local economy (Sunkel 1979, 221). As Dos

Santos (1971, 230) puts it, "Foreign capital retains control over the most dynamic sectors of the economy." Such control allows foreigners to play a major role in local politics because "the great multinational corporations . . . obviously hold the keys to the [host country] economy" (Galeano 1971, 221). This creates what is referred to as the "infrastructure of dependence," where the host government finds that it must follow the corporate lead when making its most important decisions so that unfavorable responses by major firms that might lead to severe economic problems can be avoided (Bodenheimer 1971, 162). As a result of these circumstances, international, rather than domestic, needs and interests become the guideposts to policy, for "dependency means . . . that the alternatives open to the dependent nation are defined and limited by its integration into and functions within the world market" (Bodenheimer 1971, 158).

This heavy reliance by the host government on international corporations has far-reaching consequences. One is that those who comprise the dominant local elite will come more and more to adopt foreign-inspired values and to look to foreign corporations for support in retaining political power (Mahler 1981, 272). The result is an alliance in which the foreigners are the senior partners, acting to prop up the local government and provide it with economic support in exchange for an unfettered access to local resources and labor and for government policies, such as low taxes and restrictions on labor organizations, that create a political and social climate conducive to the multiplication of corporate profits (Deyo 1981, 16). According to Galtung (1971, 83–85), this pattern of cooperation is based both on the harmony of interests between the international firm and the local elite and on the disharmony of interests between the local elite and the poverty-stricken masses found in developing societies, leading to a system that blends international control (by corporations over developing governments) with intranational dominance (by the alliance of the corporation and the government over local workers and peasants). Senghaas (1975, 275) concurs with this analysis, stating, "Today, the multinational corporations, centrally located in the different capitalist metropoles but operating globally, are the principal agents of this dynamics."

The government's close relationship with foreign firms and its extreme reliance on its corporate allies means that it is "void of any legitimacy as a ruling class" (Pinelo 1973, x). The local economy will sputter fitfully, displaying a tendency toward stagnation and negative growth rates. One of the primary goals of foreign investment in developing countries consists of preventing economic development. Baran (1957, 197) argues that "the main task of [corporate] imperialism in our time . . . [is] to prevent . . . the economic development of underdeveloped countries." Blocking economic growth in poor countries leaves their resources, labor, and capital open to exploitation by multinational firms, which means that "the development of parts of the [international] system occur at the expense of other parts" (Dos Santos 1971, 226).

Galeano (1971, 215) maintains that there is a particular concern with access to host country capital, which is "drained off by foreign interests" in order that it can finance corporate activities in other parts of the world, leaving the local economy impoverished and crippled. Bodenheimer (1971, 157), Brundenius (1972, 200), and Magdoff (1976, 217) depict the loss of local capital due to the excessive repatriation of foreign corporate profits and the refusal to invest locally as a major reason for host country economic problems.

The consequences of the foreign ability to control the host government do not end with the legitimacy problems of the government and the inability to promote economic growth but extend to the distribution of local resources. Working together with their foreign allies, the host government and its closest supporters are described as concentrating the bulk of local resources in their own hands, leading to a highly skewed distribution of incomes and land ownership patterns that leaves the wealthy with comfortable and even extravagent lifestyles, while the poor must contend with barely subsistent wages and few prospects for any improvement in their lot (Rubinson 1976, 643; Timberlake and Williams 1987, 3; London and Robinson 1989, 305). As one author says, "What results is a political and social coalition of wealthy compradores, powerful monopolists, and large landowners dedicated to the defense of the existing feudal-mercantile order" (Baran 1957, 195).

The circumstances discussed have a final implication for the political scene. This has to do with the government's excessive use of repression as a means for retaining power. Repression is necessary because the government lacks legitimacy, provides no economic progress, and refuses to share resources (Timberlake and Williams 1984, 142; 1987, 3). The end product is a "regime [that] has no real political basis in city or village, lives in continual fear of the starving and restive popular masses, and relies for its stability on Praetorian guards of relatively well kept mercenaries" (Baran 1957, 195). Bodenheimer (1971, 178) agrees that "dependent or comprador governments, subservient to foreign interests, are forced to employ overt repression."

Asymmetrical alliance theorists maintain that a large foreign investment presence in developing countries contributes to each of the deprivation mechanisms described earlier. As a result, political conflict and violence are treated as a natural outgrowth of the multinational corporate penetration of poor countries. Nicaragua under the Somozas and Haiti under the Duvaliers are cited often as examples of this sort of situation.

Malevolent Influence

Bollen (1983) and Gasiorowski (1988) note that another view of how foreign investments contribute to deprivation is presented by Cardoso (1979), Evans (1979), Duvall and Freeman (1981, 1983), and O'Donnell (1988). These scholars see developing country governments, particularly in Latin

America, as bent on the most rapid growth and development possible, regarding such progress as the government's most important social objective since it can serve to guarantee the regime's imcumbency while at the same time safeguarding the independence and security of the state by substantially increasing the resource base that the government may draw on to meet challenges at home and abroad. Speedy growth is seen as a way to provide a greater array of commercial opportunities for those who support the regime, both local and foreign, because growth and development mean new markets, access to better resources, and expanded international trade, all of which are supposed to heighten the loyalty of those who are closest to the government (Evans 1979, 48; Cardoso and Faletto 1979, 167).

Within this context, foreign capital is perceived as one of the foremost methods for achieving the goals of the government. These investments are regulated carefully by the government so that they contribute to growth in several ways. First, foreign investments substantially increase the availability of capital and technology. Second, foreigners may be directed to industries where domestic entrepreneurs are unable to operate efficently, leading to an expanded scope of economic activity and growth (Evans 1979, 119, 203). Third, a large multinational corporate presence may encourage local capitalists to engage in businesses designed to complement the foreign activities, thereby magnifying the effects of foreign investments (Evans 1979, 101–106). Finally, the taxes and royalties paid by foreigners may greatly increase the government's available resources, allowing it to play a more active role as a state entrepreneur that promotes and manages new businesses (Cardoso and Faletto 1979, 165; Evans 1979, 43–50; Duvall and Freeman 1981, 113; 1983, 573).

The government's overwhelming concern with growth and progress incline it to treat speed and efficiency as being of paramount importance and to see anything that might slow the pursuit of its goals as unacceptable. The result is a hard attitude toward social reforms and mass political participation, both of which would require the allocation of scarce resources. The people are expected to contribute to the progress of the country as a whole by being acquiescent and by allowing the regime a free hand in managing society, with harsh and repressive responses awaiting those who fail to go along with the dictates of the government (Fagen 1978, 292–295; Evans 1979, 29–31; Leonard 1980, 460).

The government's overriding concern with growth and progress has other important social and political implications. Little effort is made to insure that the benefits of economic development are made available to the people as a whole. The local social, political, and economic elites are influenced increasingly by foreign, consumption-oriented values and lifestyles and amass fortunes that set them apart from the rest of the population (Leonard 1980, 464; Mahler 1981, 272). The result is a greater marginalization of the masses, as reforms are not employed to extend the ability to consume beyond a privileged few (Jackson et al. 1978, 631; Bornschier and Ballmer-Cao 1979, 488;

O'Donnell 1988, 13). A severe maldistribution of resources builds, leading to what Jackson et al. (1978, 631) label "latent conflict," which refers to the pent-up frustration and resentment of the people as they notice that the overall pattern of economic growth is not improving their lives but has brought immense benefits to the wealthy. This is what Midlarsky's (1988, 492) "difference principle" is all about (see the discussion of relative deprivation). In the end, its close ties with foreigners supposedly rob the regime of its legitimacy among the bulk of the population and its use of repression and failure to distribute widely the fruits of progress create the circumstances that many see as bringing on trouble.

Before turning to liberal arguments, it should be noted that some theorists object to a portion of the picture described. These authors generally agree with the social and political analysis presented but dispute the contentions about how foreign investments affect growth. Bornschier et al. (1978, 653–670), Bornschier (1981, 381), Bornschier and Chase-Dunn (1985, 81), and Rubinson (1977, 4) argue that any positive effects that foreign capital may have on growth are ephemeral. Their argument centers on the notion that an early, large foreign presence means the addition of new capital, which leads to higher growth in the host society. Over time, however, these authors maintain that foreigners begin to conceptualize their holdings as a source of capital for further international expansion and will use the profits from one developing country to allow them to gain entry into another. The end result is lower long-term growth, as the capital needed to sustain development is drained away.[13]

Malevolence theorists argue that multinational corporate activities are closely associated with greater inequality of all types and with repression in developing countries, both of which are projected as resulting in more political conflict. At the same time, foreign investments are described as producing more economic growth, which some maintain is not long lasting.

The Liberal View

The liberal view starts with the same basic premise that guides those who are critical of multinational corporate activities in developing countries. This is that such firms are almost exclusively motivated by a desire to maximize the profits that they make. However, liberals draw very different conclusions about what this means for corporate behavior, for they argue that, politically, most foreign firms adhere to the practice of remaining as uninvolved as possible and that, economically, foreign investments are a spur both to local growth and to the more equitable distribution of resources.

Many liberals argue that the attempt to stay out of local political controversies occurs for two reasons. The first centers on the domestic political scene within developing countries and is found in the fact that multinational corporations realize that their foreign origins tend to make them an object of local suspicions and that any undue participation in local politics will only serve to heighten those suspicions and create an atmosphere in which the firm might not be able to conduct its business and to pursue its basic goal of making profits (Frank 1980, 41). Hence, Vernon (1976, 47) suggests that foreign investors seek "to remain as unobtrusive as possible," and Barnet and Muller (1974, 90) argue that firms attempt to appear "either as a local corporation or as a vague world entity." As a result, multinational firms are depicted as playing little, if any, role in encouraging governments to use repression against the people. Some analysts maintain that foreign investors are actually wary of repressive governments because of the potential political conflict and violence that they believe might result as a part of a backlash against such government practices (Gladwin and Walter 1980, 200–206; Billet 1991, 34).

The second reason for eschewing too much local political involvement is international. Here, the focus is on the general image that is attached to corporations that do business in developing countries that have repressive governments. As Billet (1991, 33) puts it, "Multinational corporations do not want to be associated with these countries because they might be pressured by international public opinion."[14] Corporations that maintain a significant presence in countries in which the government mistreats its population run the risk of being identified as the government's partner, which might have a very deleterious effect on the corporation's worldwide operations. The adverse publicity surrounding foreign firms in South Africa during the apartheid era serves as an example. Many authors describe multinational corporations either as nonparticipants in local politics or as seeking to soften the hard-line policies of the local government.

Other liberals argue that foreign corporations stay out of local politics because of the inherently competitive atmosphere that exists between the corporation and the host government (Becker and Sklar 1987; Schatz 1987; London and Williams 1988; Huang 1989; Rothgeb 1989b, 1990). According to this view, the corporation's primary interest is in the markets, the workforce, and the natural resources that may be acquired in any particular country. The government is described as suspicious of foreign firms because they may seek to take advantage of the government. The government is depicted as motivated by the desire to retain its legitimacy among the people it rules by promoting economic growth and maintaining a free hand to formulate policy without the appearance of corporate interference.[15]

In the context of this sort of a relationship, the resources available to the corporation and to the government and their respective intensities of involvement with each other become important determinants of the types of political, social, and economic outcomes one can expect (Dolan et al. 1982, 389). The government's primary advantages are political, centering on its sovereign right to make and enforce laws regarding the territory it rules. Of course, extreme poverty and poorly organized and weak government structures can and often do restrict the government's ability to take advantage of this resource. The important resources for the corporation pertain to the capital, the technological capabilities, and the managerial expertise that it can bring to a society that has shortages of all three of these factors of production (Rothgeb 1989b, 44).

Intensity of involvement refers to a situation in which one actor perceives that it has few options that would allow it to dispense with its partner, leading to what Richardson (1978, 14) labels a "psychology of dependence." In the government's relationship with the corporation, intensity tends to be greatest when the host society suffers from the following restrictions: poverty and a weak government. Under such conditions, the government is likely to perceive foreign firms as exceptionally vital contributors of the resources that are needed to promote the local growth and development that are so desperately needed to alleviate local misery and to shore up the government's legitimacy. This is especially the case as far as foreign manufacturing investments are concerned, for investments in this sector are often described as providing a strong boost in an area that government officials believe can be important to long-term progress (Holsti 1975, 827; Rothstein 1977, 173; Muller 1985a, 454; Rothgeb 1986b, 140).

Foreigners are depicted as enjoying their greatest advantage when they invest in manufacturing and operate in the poorest parts of the developing world. And the government is best able to hold its own, to regulate the multinationals, and to secure the most benefits for the host society when the country it rules is wealthier.

It is these relative strengths and interests of the corporation and the government that determine the political impact of foreign investments on the host society. While the corporation is best able to control poorer and weaker countries, it is not clear that they will do so because there is so little to gain from the expenditure of corporate resources that such domination would require, given the poverty of such countries (Rothgeb 1990a, 466). In wealthier parts of the developing world, the story is very different. Here, the stakes are much higher, for the potential profits are greater. As a result, there may be a temptation to intervene in local politics. The host government, however, is usually better equipped to insure that the firm's behavior does nothing to undermine the basic policy course the government has set. It is the government that determines such things as the degree to which repression is used to meet popular grievances (Huang 1989, 113–117; Rothgeb 1989b, 50–54; 1990a, 462–463). The upshot is that the size of a country's foreign presence is treated as unrelated to the political deprivation mechanisms described in this chapter.

In the economic arena, liberals see foreign investments as creating the impetus for more growth and a better distribution of resources among the entire population. Growth is increased by the contributions that foreign firms make to the pools of capital, technology, and entrepreneurial talent in developing countries. Ranis (1976, 99) maintains that foreign capital helps developing countries overcome their shortages of this key factor of production, and Frank (1980, 31) depicts foreign technology as enhancing growth by increasing the efficiency of local industrial production. Beyond this, Vernon (1971, 171) states that "foreign owned subsidies were much more than conduits of foreign capital; they were mobilizers of local resources." This mobilization is a product of the following: (1) local businesses that gain contracts as suppliers and distributors for foreigners (Reuber 1973, 151–152; Vernon 1977, 142; Frank 1980, 31); (2) the tax receipts and royalties that foreigners pay and that the government can use to promote local economic activity (Vernon 1977, 155); and (3) the dissemination of efficient foreign production techniques and management styles to local businesses (Moran 1978, 87). In each case, foreign investment enhances the use of local resources and the outcome is greater growth in the host economy.

Foreign investments are also described as encouraging a fairer distribution of local resources. For one thing, foreign corporations emphasize talent in recruiting, thereby providing opportunities for many skilled individuals who are not a part of the local elite structure. For another, a trickle-down effect is envisioned wherein the expanded resources from corporate activities provides the government the wherewithal for expanded social programs (Reuber 1973, 218; Frank 1980, 31). The efficiency gained from the use of foreign technology translates into less waste and the ability to promote more reforms over time (Gilpin 1975, 58). Greater opportunities for the disadvantaged and more social services and reforms are seen as leading to a distribution of incomes that is less skewed in favor of the wealthy.

Liberals discuss foreign investments either as unrelated to or as acting to dampen the types of political deprivation processes that are hypothesized as leading to political conflict. At the same time, these investments are viewed as helping to create a climate that encourages higher levels of growth and a better distribution of incomes. Consequently, the liberal view treats the movement of multinational corporations to the developing world as one of the safest and surest ways to insure greater domestic peace and prosperity.

SUMMARY OF FOREIGN INVESTMENT, DEPRIVATION, AND CONFLICT AND PREVIOUS RESEARCH

The controversy surrounding the role played by foreign corporations in developing countries is illustrated by the views that scholars have regarding the relationship between direct foreign investments, deprivation, and political conflict. At least three schools of thought are found in the literature, two that regard foreign investment as leading to conflict and one that does not. Asymmetrical alliance theorists treat multinational corporations as dominating the host government and inducing it to pursue policies that exploit the local population, which creates lower per capita growth, an inequitable distribution of income, disruptions in the agricultural sector, and greater levels of repression. Those who see foreign investments as having a malevolent influence on the local political scene regard foreigners as working together with the host government to promote rapid growth at the expense of an inequitable distribution of incomes, problems in the agrarian arena, and the excessive use of repression. In both cases, not only do deprivation mechanisms push people toward conflict, but the government's close association with foreign corporations robs it of its legitimacy, for it becomes so tied to foreign interests that those who are ruled no longer regard it as sufficiently local.

Liberals doubt that foreign investments play much of a role in creating conflict by producing deprivation in developing societies. Liberals see foreign investments as reducing the probability of conflict by increasing growth, reducing income inequality, and bringing greater stability to the agricultural sector, all of which have the added benefit of enhancing the government's standing with the people. Also, liberals argue that foreign investments are not related to the use of repression by the host government.

Given these arguments, it is important that one consider the findings generated by cross-national research regarding these relationships. One finds substantial bodies of literature that deal with the association between growth and inequality and political conflict and between foreign investment and growth and inequality. Since the former body of literature is extensively surveyed by Zimmermann (1983) and Lichbach (1989) and the latter is exhaustingly covered by Bornschier et al. (1978), Bornschier and Chase-Dunn (1985), and Rothgeb (1989b), there is no need to repeat that exercise here. In contrast to the many studies in these areas, one finds that the literature on the linkage between repression and agricultural disruptions and political conflict and between foreign investment dependence and domestic conflict is less developed.

Agricultural Disruptions

Beginning with the systematic empirical literature on agricultural disruptions and political conflict, one finds that while many scholars regard agrarian problems as an important source of political trouble, there have been few cross-national empirical research efforts in this area. The work on this question has centered on inequalities in the distribution of land ownership and on only one form of conflict, namely, the violence associated with rebellion.[16] One particularly important result to emerge from these efforts disputes the long-held impressions of those who believe that this sort of inequality is a potent source of trouble, for Muller and Seligson (1987) found that it is the degree of income inequality throughout society as a whole, and not land ownership patterns in the agricultural sector, that are most associated with the occurrence of violence.

As important as this study is, it leaves three questions unanswered. The first pertains to whether other types of problems in the agricultural sector (instead of inequality in land ownership), such as shifts in employment patterns, are the key to conflict. Many of the arguments presented in this chapter focus more on the commercialization of agriculture and the degree to which that process disrupted peasants' lives.[17] Land ownership may not be the major consideration. Instead, difficulties may arise from changing employment patterns. A second question has to do with the type of conflict that is associated with agricultural disruptions. As noted in Chapter 1, domestic conflict can take on at least three forms, including protest, turmoil, and internal war. Those who have examined the agrarian arena as a possible source of conflict have tended to focus only on the third of these types of conflict. The other two must be analyzed as well. Finally, it is important that one consider the role that international forces, especially direct foreign investments, play as contributors to agricultural problems and to conflict. Past researchers have failed to do this. Each of these problems will be addressed in the empirical analysis in this chapter.

Repression

The analysis of political repression and domestic conflict has produced varied results. In one of the earliest studies of this relationship, Hibbs (1973) found a strong positive association between government acts of coercion and the incidence of internal war. Further analysis by Muller (1985b), Muller and Seligson (1987), and Boswell and Dixon (1990) disputed this result by noting the existence of a curvilinear relationship between these variables such that very high and very low levels of repression are associated with less political violence while intermediate levels of repression are accompanied by higher levels of violence. Additional work by Rothgeb (1991) has indicated that while there are negligible relationships between repression and either internal war or turmoil, there is a fairly consistent negative association between repression and protest across time.

Hartman and Hsiao (1988) note that one source of the discrepancies between the results from these studies can be traced to the measurement procedures that are employed. Muller (1985b), Muller and Seligson (1987), and Boswell and Dixon (1990) use a measure of repression that is based on the evaluation of a government's respect for civil rights. Hibbs (1973) and Rothgeb (1991) employ a different operationalization, examining the frequency of government acts that are designed to suppress and control behavior that the government deems unacceptable. Beyond this, one also finds differences from one study to the next as far as sampling procedures and the measure of political conflict are concerned. For example, Rothgeb (1991) focuses exclusively on developing countries while most other researchers employ samples that include advanced states, and Muller (1985b), Muller and

Seligson (1987), and Boswell and Dixon (1990) employ a conflict measure that is based on the number of deaths from political violence while Hibbs (1973) and Rothgeb (1991) use events data. These discrepencies are considered in the empirical analysis in this chapter.

A final issue of significance has to do with the dearth of systematic studies that explore the relationship between foreign investments and repression. While many authors discuss the connection between these variables, few, with the exception of Rothgeb (1989a, 1989b), have used a cross-national research design to explore the subject systematically. The results from the work that has been done cast doubt on the claim that foreign corporations induce governments to employ repressive policies. However, this research fails to consider how regional variations (the importance of which are described) may affect this relationship. Considerable work remains.

Foreign Investments and Political Conflict

Despite the growing chorus of calls for systematic analysis of the effects of foreign investment dependence on domestic political conflict, very little attention has been paid to this area until recently (Stohl 1980, 325; Zimmermann 1983, 204–205; Gurr and Lichbach 1986, 32). As a result, one finds that the literature on the linkage between investment dependence and domestic conflict is not very well developed. For example, Rothgeb (1989a, 1990b) examines the effects of foreign investment on only one type of conflict, namely, political protest. Even when the same author expands the analysis to include the investigation of political turmoil and internal war, there is still a failure to examine what economic and political mechanisms are associated with deprivation (Rothgeb 1991).

Timberlake and Williams (1987) correct for this deficiency by looking at how a state's position as a core, semiperipheral or peripheral member of the world system affects its level of income inequality and how that relates to conflict, finding that inequality is greatest in non-core states and that this is associated with more internal war.[18] Boswell and Dixon (1990) extend this analysis by considering how foreign investment affects growth and inequality and how this is related to domestic violence, discovering that higher levels of investments are related to slower growth and more inequality and that the result is higher levels of violence.

These results, however, are not unanimous. For instance, London and Robinson (1989) argue that foreign investments are associated with violence but that growth and inequality are not intervening variables. Still more contradictory are Weede and Tiefenbach's (1981) results indicating that foreign investments are not related to inequality when one controls for a possible curvilinear relationship between average per capita income and inequality.

The results from previous research have been indeterminant. In part, this problem can be traced to such things as the sample of countries used in the research design, with Weede and Tiefenbach (1981) and Timberlake and Williams (1987) including all independent countries in their analysis while other scholars look only at developing societies. One also finds differences from one study to the next with regard to the time periods examined, the types of conflict investigated, and the measurement procedures employed.

In an attempt to clarify the situation, the present research investigates a sample of developing countries that is subdivided according to region. Three types of conflict, political protest, political turmoil, and internal war, are examined during four three-year time periods between 1967 and 1978. Finally, foreign investments in the manufacturing, agriculture, and mining sectors are included in the analysis. The use of this design should prove useful in allowing one to specify where, when, and how investment dependence affects political conflict in developing countries.

RESEARCH DESIGN

This analysis uses a cross-national design that examines eighty-four countries classified by the World Bank (1976, 1980, 1983) as underdeveloped. Data limitations precluded the study of a larger sample. The same basic design, drawing on the same sample of countries, is used throughout this book.[19] States classified by the Organization for Economic Cooperation and Development (OECD) as offshore banking centers or by the World Bank as capital exporters were not included in the sample. Offshore banking centers were omitted because, as Rothgeb (1984b, 1066) notes, the offshore activities greatly inflate foreign investment scores. The exclusion of capital exporting states is suggested by Jackman (1982, 192). The states in the data set are in Appendix A.

Standard multiple regression analysis was used to examine the hypothesized relationships. Scatterplots of the bivariate relationships between the independent and dependent variables were examined to check for nonlinear associations. No clear patterns were found.[20] Cook's D was used to check for outliers, which were omitted from the analysis when necessary. As suggested by Lewis-Beck (1980, 60), the independent and control variables were regressed on one another to test for multicollinearity. Severe problems ($R^2 > .90$) were found for saturated equations that included regional interaction terms and the variables used to create those terms. Handling this problem involved using separate regression equations to examine the effects of the interaction terms and of the variables used to create those terms.[21]

Variable Measurement

Three kinds of political conflict are included as dependent variables, namely, political protest, political turmoil, and internal war. Data from the Conflict and Peace Data Bank (COPDAB) domestic scale were employed to measure these variables.[22] The domestic file codes the political and social events occurring in the states in the data set on a scale designed to capture the type of cooperation and conflict displayed. Value 10 on this scale includes acts of political protest such as demonstrations, political strikes, and distributing antigovernment propaganda. Value 13 represents such acts of political turmoil as rioting and civil violence. Value 15 pertains to events relating to internal wars, such as terrorism, guerrilla warfare, and civil war.

The conflict scores were computed as the total number of events in each category divided by the total number of events that were coded by COPDAB for each state. Separate scores were computed for each of the time periods examined. Proportions were used to avoid situations where states with large total numbers of events have high scores even though only a small percentage of their total events may be of any particular type (Hoggard 1974).[23]

Political conflict was treated as a function of either the total stock of foreign investment in manufacturing or in agriculture. As noted, many scholars regard manufacturing investments as a key to the dependence that creates deprivation in developing countries (Muller 1985a; Rothgeb 1987, 1989b), and agricultural investments are hypothesized as a fundamental source of the agrarian social changes that are projected as producing rural conflict. Foreign investment was measured as the value in U.S. dollars of the holdings of non-nationals in the manufacturing and agricultural sectors divided by the gross domestic product (GDP) from those sectors.[24] Many researchers use this measurement procedure (Jackman 1982; Rothgeb 1989b). Appendix B lists the sources used to obtain the data for foreign investment and for all the other variables examined in this book.

The reader may recall that some scholars argue that stocks and flows of foreign investments have differing effects on developing countries, with flows having a relatively short-term positive impact, while stocks have longer-term negative effects (see the malevolence arguments associated with Bornschier and Chase-Dunn [1985]). Investigating this possibility involved developing a measure for flows. As has been discussed by many previous researchers (Dolan and Tomlin 1980, 55; Jackman 1982, 188; Rothgeb 1984–1985, 12), direct measures of inflows of new investments and the reinvestments of profits that are broken down according to sectoral location are not available. As a result, it was necessary to employ an indirect measure based on the change in the total stock of foreign investment over time. The procedure suggested by Jackman (1980, 606; 1982, 188) was used. Flows were calculated using the following continuous growth formula discussed by Taylor and Hudson (1972, 206):

$$\text{Growth} = \text{Ln}(Vtn \ / \ Vt1) \ / \ n$$

where

$$\text{Ln} = \text{natural logarithm}$$

Vtn = the value of the variable in the last year of the time period
$Vt1$ = the value of the variable in the first year of the time period
n = the number of years between $t1$ and tn

For the calculation of flows, Vtn was the value of total stocks in 1971 and $Vt1$ was the value of total stocks in 1967 (see the discussion of time periods later in this chapter). It should be noted that measuring flows by comparing stocks at two different points in time provides one with an approximation of the amount of increase or decrease in the total size of the foreign presence. Such a change only partially reflects the flows and reinvestments that occur (Rothgeb 1986b, 146). However, the dearth of data on direct investment flows leaves one with few alternatives to this sort of measure. For the most part, prior researchers who have examined flows have based their measure on the difference in stocks (Bornschier et al. 1978; Bornschier and Chase-Dunn 1985; Dolan and Tomlin 1980; Jackman 1982; Rothgeb 1984b, 1984–1985, 1986b).

The following two control variables also were included: (1) the strength of the host government and (2) the size of the host country.[25] The government's strength was included because many analysts see this variable as important for determining whether an individual will engage in conflict (Hibbs 1973, 113; Muller and Seligson 1987, 429; Tilly 1978, 158). The size of the host country is controlled for because it is seen as affecting the state's ability to regulate foreign firms (Jackman 1982; Rothgeb 1987).

Government strength was measured as total government expenditures divided by total GDP. Using central government expenditures assumes that higher spending indicates a greater role for the government. Weighting by GDP assumes that the size of a country determines the efficacy of a given level of spending. Size was measured as the total population of the host state. Population was logarithmically transformed because it is skewed.

In examining the deprivation mechanisms described, it is necessary to assess the impact of foreign investment on political conflict via a prior effect on per capita growth, income inequality, changes in the agricultural labor force, and government acts of repression. Per capita growth was measured as the average yearly real growth in GDP per capita for each of the time periods investigated.[26] Inequality was measured as the share of total income for the entire society that goes to the poorest 20 percent of the population.[27] Change in agricultural labor was computed as the difference over time in the proportion of a states' population that was employed in the agricultural sector. Operationalizing repression involved the use of COPDAB data. Hibbs (1973, 88) and Hartman and Hsiao (1988, 796) maintain that events data are most appropriate for measuring repression.[28] A proportional measure of the sort described was constructed by dividing the number of events coded as 11, 12, or 14 by the total events for each state. Scale values 11, 12, and 14 include such repressive acts as imposing curfews, forbidding public meetings, arresting opposition leaders, and imposing martial law.

Regional Variations

The empirical analysis in this chapter employs an approach that subdivides the countries in the sample according to their regional location. This is done because many researchers assert that the effects of foreign investment are not uniform but vary according to the type of host country examined, with regional location emerging as one key to distinguishing between differing types of host society.[29] Past research strongly indicates that many political phenomena vary by region. For example, Jackson and Rosberg (1982, 1) note that "state institutions and organizations are less developed in the sub-Saharan region than almost anywhere else," and Marshall (1985) found that a state's regional location emerged as the best determinant of gender politics. The same is true of how a country responds to external forces. Evans (1987) and Greenhalgh (1988) point out that Latin American countries are more penetrated than states in other regions, and Bornschier et al. (1978) and Rothgeb (1988) found that foreign investments affect economic growth in African states more than in other regions.

Based on these profiles, African states may be projected both as the most susceptible to deprivation-induced conflict and as the most likely to benefit from liberal effects because their poverty and weakness should make them easily exploited or should magnify the contribution by foreign investments of any missing factors of production. The stronger political institutions and the greater wealth in Latin America and parts of Asia should make these societies more immune to external exploitation. At the same time, these characteristics should mean that the countries in these regions will be less likely to feel any liberal benefits.

Interaction terms were used to analyze regional variations. Dummy variables were created to represent sub-Saharan African, American, and Asian countries. These variables were produced by assigning a 1 to all states in the region in question and a 0 to all others. Interaction terms were then created by multiplying the dummy variables by the foreign investment variables described. These interaction terms allowed one to compare the pattern for each region to the pattern for the rest of the states in the data set.[30]

Time Periods

In order to assess whether the relationships analyzed vary over time, the investigation was conducted for the following four time periods: 1967–1969, 1970–1972, 1973–1975, and 1976–1978.[31] These years were considered particularly pertinent for analyzing changes because they include periods during which the economic performance throughout the entire world and in the specific regions highlighted in this study varied substantially. As is clear from examining Table 2.1, 1967–1969 and 1970–1972 generally were periods of solid growth both in per capita terms and in industry all over the globe. The only exception to this is in East Asia, where per capita income stagnated in 1970–1972. However, 1973–1975 and 1976–1978 display slower and even negative growth rates. This is especially the case in 1973–1975, with 1976–1978 appearing as a time of mild recovery.

Given these differences in economic performance, the examination of these four time periods allows one to assess claims that changes in the international economic climate have an effect on the economic health and social stability of developing countries (Krasner 1976, 319; Gasiorowski 1985, 341; Clark 1989, 173). In particular, one can investigate the degree to which a poor country's linkages to the international system by way of foreign investment affect both its economic and social prospects and its level of political conflict during periods of economic prosperity (1967–1969 and 1970–1972), recession (1973–1975), and recovery (1976–1978).[32]

In operationalizing the variables in this analysis, the dependent (protest, turmoil, and internal war) and intervening (growth, inequality, repression, and change in the agricultural labor force) variables were measured for each of the four time periods. The only exceptions to this were the measures of in-

Table 2.1
World and Regional per Capita and Industrial Growth Rates, 1967–1978

	1967–69	1970–72	1973–75	1976–78
Per Capita Growth				
World	3.8	3.4	-0.9	2.4
Developed Market Economies	3.8	3.4	-1.3	2.8
Africa	3.9	2.5	0.9	2.4
Latin America and Caribbean	3.3	3.9	2.2	2.4
East and Southeast Asia	3.8	0.0	1.4	5.2
Industrial Growth				
World	7.8	5.4	-0.4	5.1
Developed Market Economies	7.1	4.4	-4.0	5.0
Africa	12.9	4.9	-2.7	4.0
Latin America and Caribbean	8.7	7.7	3.3	4.9
East and Southeast Asia	10.4	7.2	5.1	9.0

Note: The figures for Africa exclude South Africa and those for East and Southeast Asia exclude Japan.

equality and change in the agricultural labor force. The income inequality data from the World Bank only were available for the 1965–1970 period, with the actual date varying somewhat from one country to the next. The data needed to compute changes in the agricultural labor force only were available for 1965, 1970, 1975, and 1980. Therefore, the differences from 1965 to 1970 were used to approximate the measure for 1967–1969, the differences from 1970–1975 approximated 1970–1972 and 1973–1975, and the differences from 1975–1980 approximated 1976–1978.

The remaining variables in the analysis were measured for 1967–1969. Foreign investment data broken down according to sectoral location only were available for 1967.[33] Government expenditures and total population were measured for 1967. As indicated earlier, flows of foreign investment were measured for 1967–1971 because these were the years for which data were available that best approximated the current needs. These measurement procedures were patterned after those that Rothgeb (1986a) employed in his analysis of how international economic conditions affect foreign investment in developing countries.

RESULTS

Absolute Deprivation

The investigation of absolute deprivation rested on the association between manufacturing investments, flows of foreign investments, per capita growth, and political conflict.[34] Examining these relationships involved analyzing multiple sets of regression equations (Asher 1976, 11–20).[35] The first considered the effect of foreign investment (either stocks or flows) on per capita growth as follows:

$$\text{GDP per cap} = a + b1 \text{ ForInv} + b2 \text{ Pop} + b3 \text{ GovExp} + e$$

The effects of the interaction terms were investigated by substituting each of those variables separately for ForInv in this equation.[36]

A second set of equations considered the relationship between foreign investment, per capita growth, and political conflict. It is as follows:

$$\text{PolCon} = a + b1 \text{ ForInv} + b2 \text{ GDP per cap} + b3 \text{ Pop} + b4 \text{ GovExp} + e$$

The examination of the interaction terms used the same substitutions mentioned above.

Table 2.2 reports the results for the association between manufacturing investments, flows of foreign investments, and per capita growth. The results show that among African states there are negative relationships between manufacturing investments and growth during the 1973–1975 and 1976–1978

Table 2.2
Foreign Investments and per Capita Growth

Time Period	ForInv	Amer x ForInv	Afr x ForInv	Asia x ForInv	Pop	GovExp	R2	N
			Stocks of Manufacturing Investments					
	.21				.28	.17	.10	56
1967–		-.16			.17	.14	.08	56
1969			.22		.26	.17	.10	56
				-.06	.23	.15	.06	56
	-.07				.14	.01	.03	58
1970–		.20			.21	.04	.06	58
1972			-.25		.11	-.01	.08	58
				.15	.12	.02	.05	58
	-.14				-.02	.02	.02	57
1973–		.37b			.11	.07	.13	57
1975			-.36b		-.05	.00	.12	57
				.16	-.02	.03	.03	57
	-.26				.08	.08	.09	55
1976–		.19			.19	.12	.06	55
1978			-.39b		.07	.06	.17	55
				.22	.09	.10	.07	55
			Flows of Foreign Investments					
	.17				.19	.16	.08	54
1967–		.02			.21	.13	.05	54
1969			.20		.20	.12	.09	54
				.21	.15	.15	.09	54
	.48c				.08	.10	.23	56
1970–		.27a			.15	.01	.09	56
1972			.08		.13	-.01	.02	56
				.40b	.03	.03	.17	56
	.28a				-.04	.09	.08	55
1973–		.18			.00	.04	.04	55
1975			-.01		-.01	.03	.00	55
				.29a	-.09	.05	.08	55
	.23				.13	.12	.08	53
1976–		.07			.16	.07	.03	53
1978			.14		.15	.06	.04	53
				.29a	.08	.09	.10	53

Note: Beta weights are reported. a p<.05, b p<.01, c p<.001, d p<.0001

time periods. American states display a different pattern, with a positive association between manufacturing investments and growth in 1973–1975. There is no apparent relationship between stock of manufacturing investments and growth either for Asian countries or for the sample as a whole. The control variables also appear unrelated to growth.

A consideration of the results for flows reveals a very different story. Here one finds a positive relationship between flows and growth throughout the 1970s for Asian countries. One also finds a positive relationship for the entire sample in 1970–1972 and 1973–1975 and for American states in 1970–1972. Higher flows are related to greater levels of growth, with the effects centering primarily on Asian states during the years 1970–1978. Once again, the control variables are not related to growth.

It would appear from these patterns both that stocks and flows of foreign investments have very different effects on growth and that these effects vary from one developing region to another. For stocks, the effect on growth appears greatest during periods of international recession. Among the very poor countries in Africa, stocks seem to exacerbate the effects of international economic disturbances, for they are associated with slower growth rates at precisely the moment when these countries need an economic engine to compensate for international downturns. In the Americas, however, the effects are the opposite, for stocks apparently cushion these countries from the untoward effects of international difficulties. As for flows, the primary effects are found in Asia, where they are associated with higher growth during periods of prosperity (1970–1972) and recession (1973–1975).

Having established the patterns of relationships between foreign investments and growth, it is now possible to consider the effects on political conflict. Table 2.3 has the results for internal war when growth is in the equation. Looking first at the effects of growth on internal war, one finds that lower growth is associated with higher conflict during the 1976–1978 period. If one reflects on the previous results from Table 2.2, one can discern both a deprivation pattern for African states and a liberal pattern for Asian countries. Among African countries, foreign manufacturing investments are associated with lower growth, which is in turn related to more internal war. For Asian states, flows of foreign investments are related to higher growth, which is associated with less internal war. These patterns only apply, however, to the latter part of the 1970s when the international system was experiencing a time of stagnant economic growth.

As far as foreign investment is concerned, the results reveal no direct results. The same is true for the control variables.

Table 2.4 has the results for the relationships between foreign investments, growth, and political turmoil. In general, none of the equations displays any strong associations between either growth or foreign investment and turmoil. The only relationship of interest is the negative association between stocks of manufacturing investments and turmoil among African states in 1970–1972. However, one may conclude that this form of conflict is not affected by any discernible sort of absolute deprivation effects.

Table 2.5 has the findings for political protest. Growth has only a weak positive relationship with protest during 1970–1972 and 1973–1975, indicating that higher growth is related to more protest rather than less, as would be the case if a deprivation mechanism was at work. Therefore, one can conclude

Table 2.3
Foreign Investments, Growth, and Internal War

Time Period	ForInv	Amer x ForInv	Afr x ForInv	Asia x ForInv	Growth	Pop	GovExp	R2	N
			Stocks of Manufacturing Investments						
	-.01				-.19	-.09	-.13	.07	56
1967-		.22			-.16	-.03	-.11	.12	56
1969			-.05		-.18	-.10	-.14	.07	56
				.26	-.21	.00	-.17	.13	56
	-.08				.05	-.21	.10	.06	58
1970-		-.04			.06	-.20	.10	.05	58
1972			.03		.06	-.19	.11	.05	58
				-.17	.08	-.15	.10	.08	58
	-.02				-.17	-.11	.18	.08	57
1973-		.23			-.24	-.04	.21	.12	57
1975			-.05		-.18	-.12	.17	.08	57
				-.01	-.16	-.10	.18	.08	57
	-.16				-.47c	-.13	.00	.23	55
1976-		.08			-.45b	-.07	.02	.21	55
1978			-.17		-.50c	-.12	.00	.23	55
				-.12	-.41b	-.06	.00	.22	55
			Flows of Foreign Investment						
	-.06				-.16	-.08	-.16	.07	54
1967-		-.02			-.17	-.09	-.15	.07	54
1969			.15		-.21	-.09	-.15	.09	54
				-.11	-.15	-.06	-.16	.08	54
	-.17				.17	-.20	-.06	.07	56
1970-		-.09			.12	-.21	-.03	.05	56
1972			.10		.09	-.21	-.03	.06	56
				-.17	.16	-.17	-.04	.07	56
	-.01				-.13	-.13	.09	.05	55
1973-		-.08			-.12	-.14	.09	.05	55
1975			.04		-.13	-.14	.09	.05	55
				-.05	-.12	-.12	.09	.05	55
	-.08				-.33a	-.14	-.08	.17	53
1976-		-.04			-.35a	-.15	-.06	.16	53
1978			-.13		-.33a	-.14	-.05	.18	53
				-.03	-.34a	-.14	-.06	.16	53

Note: Beta weights are reported. a p<.05, b p<.01, c p<.001, d p<.0001

that there is little evidence to support the contention that foreign investment affects protest as a result of absolute deprivation.

Perhaps the most interesting results in Table 2.5 are those for the direct relationships between stocks of manufacturing investments and protest. The basic patterns that emerge indicate that manufacturing investments are associated with more protest among American states (at least in 1967–1969 and 1973–1975),

Table 2.4
Foreign Investments, Growth, and Turmoil

Time Period	ForInv	Amer x ForInv	Afr x ForInv	Asia x ForInv	Growth	Pop	GovExp	R2	N
			Stocks of Manufacturing Investments						
	-.19				-.06	.09	-.16	.09	56
1967–		.08			-.09	.18	-.14	.07	56
1969			-.14		-.07	.12	-.16	.08	56
				-.16	-.11	.21	-.17	.08	56
	-.14				.09	-.14	.09	.05	58
1970–		.05			.10	-.08	.11	.03	58
1972			-.29a		.04	-.15	.07	.11	58
				.02	.11	-.10	.10	.03	58
	.02				-.11	.05	-.07	.02	57
1973–		.00			-.11	.06	-.07	.02	57
1975			-.05		-.13	.05	-.08	.02	57
				.13	-.13	.02	-.07	.04	57
	.03				-.05	.28	.07	.07	55
1976–		.14			-.08	.31a	.09	.09	55
1978			-.15		-.12	.25	.07	.09	55
				.14	-.09	.24	.08	.09	55
			Flows of Foreign Investments						
	-.08				-.05	.16	-.18	.06	54
1967–		-.13			-.06	.14	-.17	.07	54
1969			.18		-.10	.15	-.17	.09	54
				-.12	-.04	.18	-.17	.07	54
	-.19				.17	-.04	-.15	.05	56
1970–		-.13			.13	-.06	-.12	.04	56
1972			.01		.09	-.05	-.11	.02	56
				-.22	.17	-.01	-.13	.06	56
	.00				-.09	.07	-.10	.03	55
1973–		-.03			-.08	.07	-.10	.03	55
1975			.04		-.09	.07	-.10	.03	55
				-.10	-.06	.10	-.11	.03	55
	.02				-.09	.30a	-.04	.10	53
1976–		-.03			-.09	.30a	-.05	.10	53
1978			.08		-.10	.30a	-.05	.10	53
				-.14	-.05	.33a	-.06	.11	53

Note: Beta weights are reported. a p<.05, b p<.01, c p<.001, d p<.0001

while the same investments in African states are related to fewer protests. The results for American countries suggest that a nondeprivation sort of mechanism may be at work. This possibility is explored in more detail.

As they apply to African states, these findings constitute evidence that can be interpreted as supporting the liberal view. One should note that the negative relationship between foreign investments and protest exists without intervening

Table 2.5
Foreign Investments, Growth, and Protest

Time Period	ForInv	Amer x ForInv	Afr x ForInv	Asia x ForInv	Growth	Pop	GovExp	R2	N
			Stock of Manufacturing Investments						
	-.30a				.10	-.10	-.40b	.22	56
1967-		.40b			.10	.09	-.33b	.28	56
1969			-.46c		.14	-.11	-.42c	.33	56
				.06	.04	-.01	-.36b	.14	56
	-.21				.24	.09	-.26a	.22	58
1970-		.20			.22	.21	-.22	.21	58
1972			-.32a		.18	.10	-.28a	.27	58
				-.08	.27a	.17	-.25	.18	58
	-.08				.24	.16	-.17	.14	57
1973-		.34a			.14	.27a	-.12	.23	57
1975			-.27a		.16	.13	-.19	.20	57
				-.18	.28a	.23	-.17	.17	57
	-.12				.12	.07	.11	.06	55
1976-		.26			.10	.17	.15	.11	55
1978			-.36a		.01	.04	.09	.15	55
				-.27	.21	.16	.10	.11	55
			Flows of Foreign Investments						
	.25				-.02	-.03	-.28a	.17	54
1967-		.14			.02	-.01	-.33a	.13	54
1969			.16		-.01	-.01	-.35a	.14	54
				.20	-.02	-.06	-.32a	.15	54
	.05				.22	.13	-.23	.16	56
1970-		-.06			.26	.12	-.24	.16	56
1972			.05		.24	.13	-.25	.16	56
				.06	.22	.12	-.25	.16	56
	.15				.24	.15	-.22	.20	55
1973-		.12			.26a	.17	-.25	.19	55
1975			.17		.28a	.16	-.27a	.21	55
				.06	.26	.15	-.25	.18	55
	.12				.11	.16	.00	.07	53
1976-		.18			.13	.18	-.02	.09	53
1978			.07		.13	.17	-.03	.06	53
				-.07	.16	.19	-.03	.06	53

Note: Beta weights are reported. a $p<.05$, b $p<.01$, c $p<.001$, d $p<.0001$

linkages for growth. As is mentioned, liberals expect reduced conflict to come from economic improvements. The absence of a connection by way of growth suggests that for at least one type of conflict, protest, the liberal view of how manufacturing investments affect conflict should be modified to allow for the possibility of a direct effect that lowers the probability of conflict. This reduction may stem from the general air of credibility and confidence that are attached to governments in societies that have higher levels of foreign investments, which may be perceived as an international endorsement of the government and which may create the impression that things in society are moving in the right direction. It is interesting to note that these effects are confined to the poorer and more newly independent African states.

The results pertaining to absolute deprivation indicate that stocks of manufacturing investments are associated with lower levels of per capita economic growth and that this is related to higher levels of domestic conflict. This pattern only affects one region (Africa) and one type of conflict (internal war) under one set of international conditions (periods of stagnation and very mild recovery). At the same time, flows of foreign investment in Asia seem to produce liberal effects, for in this region higher flows are associated with higher growth, which in turn appears to dampen the probability of internal war.

Relative Deprivation

The examination of relative deprivation involved analyzing the relationships between foreign investment, income inequality, and political conflict. The following first set of regression equations used for this purpose looked at the effect of foreign investment on income inequality:[37]

$$\text{Income} = a + b1 \text{ ForInv} + b2 \text{ Pop} + b3 \text{ GovExp} + e$$

The following second equations focused on the relationships between foreign investment, inequality, and political conflict:

$$\text{PolCon} = a + b1 \text{ ForInv} + b2 \text{ Income} + b3 \text{ Pop} + b4 \text{ GovExp} + e$$

The interaction terms were substituted into these equations as described.

Table 2.6 has the results for the association between foreign investments and income inequality. These findings show that among American states, higher manufacturing investments are associated with lower income shares for the poorest 20 percent of the population. Countries in the other two regions that were examined display no pattern of relationships between these variables. The same is true of the control variables.

Turning to the effects on conflict, one finds the results for internal war in Table 2.7. These findings show that reduced income shares for the poor are strongly related to higher levels of internal war during the prosperity found in 1967–1969. The patterns for the remaining variables in the equations are much the same as they were in Table 2.3, with the foreign investment variables displaying few direct effects on internal war.

When one juxtaposes the results in Table 2.7 with those in Table 2.6, one finds support for the proposition that manufacturing investments in the Americas are associated with relative deprivation-based conflict that is derived from inequality. These effects, however, are limited to American states and seem to

Table 2.6
Foreign Investments and Income Inequality

	ForInv	Amer x ForInv	Afr x ForInv	Asia x ForInv	Pop	GovExp	R2	N
Stock of Manufacturing Investments								
	-.18				.18	-.06	.10	43
		-.45b			.09	-.14	.25	43
			.18		.30	-.05	.11	43
				.11	.22	-.06	.09	43
Stock of Agricultural Investments								
	-.11				.22	-.05	.09	45
		-.12			.22	-.05	.09	45
			.08		.27	-.07	.09	45
				-.03	.26	-.06	.08	45

Note: Beta weights are reported. a p<.05, b p<.01, c p<.001, d p<.0001

Table 2.7
Manufacturing Investments, Income Inequality, and Internal War

Time Period	ForInv	Amer x ForInv	Afr x ForInv	Asia x ForInv	Income	Pop	GovExp	R2	N
	-.11				-.55c	-.05	-.21	.31	43
1967–		.00			-.53b	-.01	-.20	.30	43
1969			-.05		-.52c	-.03	-.20	.31	43
				-.14	-.52c	.02	-.20	.32	43
	-.42a				-.19	-.29	.14	.23	43
1970–		-.06			-.15	-.14	.15	.09	43
1972			-.29		-.07	-.21	.17	.16	43
				-.12	-.11	-.09	.17	.10	43
	-.03				-.29	-.17	.29	.26	43
1973–		.16			-.22	-.12	.33a	.28	43
1975			-.12		-.27	-.19	.29a	.27	43
				.11	-.30a	-.19	.29	.27	43
	-.26				-.32a	-.29	-.10	.19	43
1976–		-.18			-.34a	-.24	-.12	.16	43
1978			-.08		-.26	-.21	-.09	.14	43
				-.19	-.25	-.13	-.08	.17	43

Note: Beta weights are reported. a p<.05, b p<.01, c p<.001, d p<.0001

occur only when the international system is experiencing a period of economic growth.

The results for political turmoil and political protest in Tables 2.8 and 2.9 display no patterns of association between inequality and either of these forms of conflict. One does find that among African states there is a direct negative relationship between manufacturing investments and turmoil in 1970–1972 and 1976–1978. There also is a negative relationship between these investments and political protest in each of the time periods examined. These patterns are similar to those found between these variables in Tables 2.4 and 2.5.

Among the control variables, the most notable relationships are the strong negative effects of government expenditures on both of these types of conflict. The effects on turmoil are limited to 1970–1972, but those for protest are more general, affecting every time period except 1976–1978. This indicates that stronger governments with greater pools of resources are better able to discourage and control these types of conflict.

Agrarian Deprivation

The effects of agrarian deprivation were examined by considering the relationships between foreign investments in agriculture, the change over time in

Table 2.8
Manufacturing Investments, Income Inequality, and Turmoil

Time Period	ForInv	Amer x ForInv	Afr x ForInv	Asia x ForInv	Income	Pop	GovExp	R2	N
1967–1969	-.19				.04	-.08	-.30	.12	43
		.10			.11	.02	-.27	.10	43
			-.15		.10	-.05	-.29	.12	43
				-.11	.08	.03	-.29	.11	43
1970–1972	-.42b				-.11	-.40a	-.36a	.28	43
		.00			-.05	-.23	-.34a	.13	43
			-.52c		.05	-.39b	-.33a	.39	43
				.19	-.07	-.30	-.34a	.17	43
1973–1975	-.16				-.01	-.03	-.11	.03	43
		-.16			-.05	-.01	-.13	.03	43
			.02		.01	.03	-.10	.01	43
				.21	-.01	-.03	-.11	.05	43
1976–1978	-.18				-.21	.18	-.19	.15	43
		.02			-.17	.26	-.17	.12	43
			-.36a		-.11	.15	-.17	.24	43
				.28	-.21	.17	-.19	.19	43

Note: Beta weights are reported. a p<.05, b p<.01, c p<.001, d p<.0001

Table 2.9
Manufacturing Investments, Income Inequality, and Protest

Time Period	ForInv	Amer x ForInv	Afr x ForInv	Asia x ForInv	Income	Pop	GovExp	R2	N
	-.01				-.19	-.07	-.47b	.23	43
1967-		.26			-.08	.00	-.42b	.28	43
1969			-.31a		-.13	-.15	-.47b	.32	43
				.03	-.19	-.07	-.47b	.24	43
	-.11				-.07	.06	-.35a	.15	43
1970-		.14			.00	.14	-.31	.16	43
1972			-.43b		.02	-.02	-.34a	.31	43
				-.08	-.05	.13	-.34a	.15	43
	.05				-.15	.11	-.41a	.20	43
1973-		.35a			-.01	.18	-.34a	.28	43
1975			-.36a		-.09	-.02	-.40b	.31	43
				-.09	-.15	.11	-.41b	.20	43
	-.14				-.23	.03	-.23	.11	43
1976-		.30			-.08	.16	-.16	.15	43
1978			-.52c		-.11	-.07	-.22	.34	43
				-.25	-.18	.16	-.22	.14	43

Note: Beta weights are reported. a p<.05, b p<.01, c p<.001, d p<.0001

the proportion of the population employed in the agricultural sector, and political conflict. The first regression equation that follows investigated the effects of agricultural investments on the change in the agricultural labor force:

$$AgLab = a + b1 \text{ ForInv} + b2 \text{ Pop} + b3 \text{ GovExp} + e$$

The second equation that follows considered the effects of agricultural investments and change in the agricultural labor force on conflict:

$$PolCon = a + b1 \text{ ForInv} + b2 \text{ AgLab} = b3 \text{ Pop} + b4 \text{ GovExp} + e$$

The same substitutions for the interaction terms that were used were employed in these equations.

Table 2.10 has the results for the association between foreign investments and change in the agricultural labor force. There is a positive relationship between agricultural investments and change in agricultural labor during 1965–1970 and 1975–1980 for African states. There is a similar relationship for the entire sample in 1965–1970. These results indicate that agricultural investments are associated with the retention of workers in agrarian activities, suggesting that these investments have effects that parallel those described by

Table 2.10
Agricultural Investments and Change in the Agricultural Labor Force

Time Period	ForInv	Amer x ForInv	Afr x ForInv	Asia x ForInv	Pop	GovExp	R2	N
1965–1970	.27a				.07	-.08	.08	59
		-.03			-.01	-.08	.01	59
			.42b		-.01	-.12	.18	59
				.11	-.05	-.03	.02	59
1970–1975	-.22				-.13	-.23	.11	59
		-.17			-.16	-.27	.08	59
			.23		-.09	-.23	.10	59
				.15	-.08	-.25	.09	59
1970–1975	.13				-.07	-.26	.08	58
		-.16			-.15	-.30a	.09	58
			.27a		-.06	-.32a	.14	58
				.15	-.10	-.27a	.10	58

Note: Beta weights are reported. a p<.05, b p<.01, c p<.001, d p<.0001

liberals, especially in the very poor countries of sub-Saharan Africa. There are no apparent effects in the other regions examined.

Government expenditures is the only control variable related to the change in agricultural labor, with a negative effect in 1975–1980, implying that during this period of time, larger governments may have been inclined to shift workers out of the agricultural sector.

Having established the patterns of relationships between foreign investments and change in agricultural labor, it is now possible to consider the effects on political conflict. Table 2.11 has the results for internal war. There are no associations between any of the variables in the analysis and internal war. This is true across each of the three regions and the four time periods that were investigated. Foreign investments in agriculture and changes in agrarian labor are not associated with this form of conflict. Interestingly, these findings extend and support the results found by Muller and Seligson (1987), who reported that agrarian land ownership patterns were not related to a society's level of violence. The findings herein suggest strongly that other forms of agrarian change are not as responsible for highly violent conflict as some authors have argued.[38]

The findings for turmoil are in Table 2.12. There is no relationship between changes in agricultural labor and this form of conflict in any of the periods investigated. As far as foreign investments are concerned, African states have a negative relationship in 1970–1972 and 1976–1978 and American states display a positive association in 1970–1972. There also is a mild positive relationship for the entire sample in 1973–1975. These results indicate that,

Table 2.11
Agricultural Investments, Change in the Agricultural Labor Force, and Internal War

Time Period	ForInv	Amer x ForInv	Afr x ForInv	Asia x ForInv	AgLab	Pop	GovExp	R2	N
	-.11				.00	-.21	-.09	.05	58
1967-		.07			-.10	-.12	-.15	.06	58
1969			-.04		-.19	-.12	-.21	.08	58
				-.10	-.11	-.12	-.18	.06	58
	-.15				.14	-.22	.19	.11	58
1970-		.23			.12	-.14	.08	.10	58
1972			-.12		.17	-.19	.20	.11	58
				-.14	.19	-.17	.20	.11	58
	-.10				.17	-.17	.09	.07	58
1973-		.19			.14	-.14	-.01	.08	58
1975			-.23		.17	-.17	.26	.14	58
				-.11	.15	-.17	.10	.07	58
	-.11				.04	-.24	-.11	.07	58
1976-		.07			.04	-.19	-.09	.06	58
1978			-.11		.10	-.14	-.08	.05	58
				-.13	.06	-.17	-.12	.06	58

Note: Beta weights are reported. a p<.05, b p<.01, c p<.001, d p<.0001

Table 2.12
Agricultural Investments, Change in the Agricultural Labor Force, and Turmoil

Time Period	ForInv	Amer x ForInv	Afr x ForInv	Asia x ForInv	AgLab	Pop	GovExp	R2	N
	.03				.02	.10	-.15	.04	58
1967-		.18			.04	.15	-.11	.07	58
1969			.11		-.19	.09	-.17	.06	58
				-.11	-.13	.09	-.14	.07	58
	.07				.02	.09	-.08	.02	58
1970-		.40b			-.02	.11	-.02	.15	58
1972			-.39b		-.01	.03	-.01	.16	58
				.19	-.12	-.06	-.13	.05	58
	.28a				.10	.15	-.07	.09	58
1973-		.04			.21	.14	-.12	.08	58
1975			-.05		.22	.13	-.11	.09	58
				-.20	.11	.11	-.14	.08	58
	.11				.10	.40b	-.04	.16	58
1976-		.10			.13	.40b	.00	.16	58
1978			-.26a		.15	.32a	.01	.19	58
				.18	.11	.42b	.00	.23	58

Note: Beta weights are reported. a p<.05, b p<.01, c p<.001, d p<.0001

with the exception of the recessionary years of 1973–1975, in African countries in the 1970s, agricultural investments had the dampening effect on political turmoil that liberals describe. Foreign investments seem to exert their effect on this form of conflict more through some sort of social and political influences on the host society than by altering economic circumstances.

Population is the only control variable related to turmoil, with a positive association in 1976–1978. Apparently larger countries experienced higher levels of turmoil during the period of international recovery found in 1976–1978.

The findings for protest are in Table 2.13. Looking first at the effects of agricultural labor changes, one finds a consistent negative relationship between this variable and protest. The only exceptions are found in 1970–1972 (although even here there is an effect when one examines the African equation) and in the American equations for 1967–1969 and 1976–1978. Basically, these results strongly suggest that throughout much of the developing world, the retention of workers in their patterns of agrarian employment means that there will be fewer acts of political protest. When juxtaposed with the results in Table 2.10, one finds support for liberal conceptions of how agricultural investments affect the prospects for conflict in poor countries by way of their prior effect on agricultural employment.

Table 2.13
Agricultural Investments, Change in the Agricultural Labor Force, and Protest

Time Period	ForInv	Amer x ForInv	Afr x ForInv	Asia x ForInv	AgLab	Pop	GovExp	R2	N
	.34b				-.43c	.15	-.46c	.35	58
1967–		.20			-.23	.14	-.32a	.23	58
1969			-.22		-.30a	.03	-.38b	.29	58
				.04	-.34b	.04	-.41b	.25	58
	.01				-.20	.13	-.31a	.13	58
1970–		.35b			-.19	.28	-.19	.26	58
1972			-.29a		-.30a	.16	-.20	.25	58
				-.09	-.19	.14	-.30a	.14	58
	.16				-.40b	.21	-.33b	.32	58
1973–		.27a			-.33b	.28a	-.31a	.34	58
1975			-.13		-.45c	.15	-.29a	.31	58
				-.10	-.43c	.16	-.30a	.31	58
	.05				-.42b	.14	-.16	.19	58
1976–		.38b			-.25	.30a	-.01	.25	58
1978			-.25		-.35a	.11	-.09	.25	58
				-.15	-.40b	.14	-.14	.21	58

Note: Beta weights are reported. a p<.05, b p<.01, c p<.001, d p<.0001

Table 2.13 also reveals that agricultural investments have direct effects on protest. Among American states, there is a consistent positive relationship between foreign investment and protest after 1967–1969. More investments are associated with greater conflict. Interestingly, this pattern is found only among the more highly developed and older societies of Latin America. It is possible that this relationship represents a nationalist backlash of some sort against foreign penetration of an area of the economy that is often seen as a key part of a society's heritage. This will be explored in more detail in Chapter 4.

With the exception of a negative relationship for African states in 1970–1972, there are no relationships between foreign agricultural investments and protest in the other regions. Among the control variables, government strength is negatively related to protest in 1967–1969 and 1973–1975. Also, there is a positive association for population in the American equations in every time period except 1967–1969, implying that in this region, larger states tended to experience more protest throughout the 1970s.

Political Deprivation

The analysis of political deprivation was based on an examination of the relationships between foreign investment, repression, and political conflict. The first regression equation used to do this looked at the effect of foreign manufacturing investments on repression as follows:

$$\text{Repress} = a + b1\ \text{ForInv} + b2\ \text{Pop} + b3\ \text{GovExp} + e$$

The second equation investigated the effects of foreign investment and repression on conflict as follows:

$$\text{PolCon} = a + b1\ \text{ForInv} + b2\ \text{Repress} + b3\ \text{Pop} + b4\ \text{GovExp} + e$$

Once again, the interaction terms were substituted into these equations when appropriate.

The effects of foreign investment on repression are displayed in Table 2.14. Here one finds a negative relationship between manufacturing investments and repression for American states in 1967–1969 and 1973–1975. There also is a negative relationship for the entire sample of developing countries in 1967–1969. There is no relationship between foreign investments and repression in either Africa or Asia. These findings suggest that among American states, foreign manufacturing investments have a liberalizing effect, particularly during the periods of international prosperity found in the late 1960s and during the recessionary years of the mid-1970s. Future research should explore the reasons why these liberal effects are found during these specific time periods.

As far as the control variables are concerned, only government expenditures are related to repression. The results reveal that in 1967–1969 stronger

Table 2.14
Manufacturing Investments and Repression

Time Period	ForInv	Amer x ForInv	Afr x ForInv	Asia x ForInv	Pop	GovExp	R2	N
	-.32a				-.11	.31a	.21	58
1967-		-.32a			-.10	.29a	.20	58
1969			-.19		-.06	.31a	.14	58
				.02	-.02	.33a	.11	58
	-.18				.00	.00	.03	58
1970-		-.11			.02	.00	.01	58
1972			-.08		.03	.01	.01	58
				-.03	.06	.01	.00	58
	-.07				-.11	.04	.02	58
1973-		-.34a			-.17	.00	.12	58
1975			.01		-.09	.05	.01	58
				.21	-.14	.05	.05	58
	-.22				-.04	-.24	.10	58
1976-		-.19			-.02	-.25	.09	58
1978			-.09		.01	-.24	.06	58
				-.04	.04	-.23	.06	58

Note: Beta weights are reported. a p<.05, b p<.01, c p<.001, d p<.0001

governments engaged in a greater use of repression. There are no effects during the other time periods examined.

Turning to the effects on conflict, one finds in Table 2.15 that repression is not related to internal war.[39] In fact, the only relationship found in this table is the positive effect of foreign investments on internal war among American states during the 1967–1969 period. These results cast strong doubt on the often-found claims that multinational corporations are responsible for high level conflict by way of a prior impact on the government's use of repression.

The results in Table 2.16 reinforce the impression from Table 2.15 that a large foreign investment presence does not lead to violence by way of increased government repression, for one finds here that repression is only related to conflict during the late 1970s and that the effect is negative instead of positive. There are no additional relationships other than those that were found in earlier tables that show that foreign investments in Africa are negatively related to turmoil in 1970–1972 and that states with larger populations tended to experience less conflict in 1976–1978.

Table 2.17 completes the picture regarding the relationship between foreign investments, repression, and conflict by providing the results for protest. Repression appears to have no effect on this form of conflict. The only results found in this table conform closely to those that were reported previously for foreign investments in Africa and in America and for government expenditures.

Table 2.15
Manufacturing Investments, Repression, and Internal War

Time Period	ForInv	Amer x ForInv	Afr x ForInv	Asia x ForInv	Repress	Pop	GovExp	R2	N
1967–1969	-.04				.03	-.13	-.18	.04	58
		.30a			.14	-.04	-.18	.11	58
			-.09		.02	-.14	-.19	.04	58
				-.21	.05	-.06	-.19	.08	58
1970–1972	-.08				-.01	-.21	.10	.06	58
		-.02			.00	-.19	.10	.05	58
			.01		.01	-.18	.11	.05	58
				-.16	.00	-.14	.10	.07	58
1973–1975	.00				-.11	-.13	.17	.06	58
		.12			-.07	-.10	.18	.07	58
			.01		-.11	-.13	.17	.07	58
				-.01	-.10	-.13	.17	.06	58
1976–1978	-.05				-.05	-.12	-.11	.02	58
		-.03			-.05	-.11	-.11	.02	58
			.02		-.04	-.10	-.10	.02	58
				-.22	-.05	-.05	-.12	.06	58

Note: Beta weights are reported. a p<.05, b p<.01, c p<.001, d p<.0001

Table 2.16
Manufacturing Investments, Repression, and Turmoil

Time Period	ForInv	Amer x ForInv	Afr x ForInv	Asia x ForInv	Repress	Pop	GovExp	R2	N
1967–1969	-.23				-.13	.07	-.14	.10	58
		.11			-.01	.16	-.15	.07	58
			-.16		-.08	.10	-.16	.08	58
				-.16	-.05	.17	-.16	.08	58
1970–1972	-.19				-.18	-.13	.09	.07	58
		.05			-.14	-.06	.11	.04	58
			-.32a		-.17	-.14	.07	.13	58
				.03	-.14	-.08	.10	.04	58
1973–1975	-.02				-.13	.05	-.06	.03	58
		-.09			-.15	.03	-.07	.03	58
			-.01		-.13	.05	-.06	.03	58
				.13	-.15	.02	-.06	.04	58
1976–1978	-.02				-.28a	.27a	-.01	.14	
		.06			-.26	.30a	.00	.15	58
			-.12		-.29a	.26	-.03	.16	58
				.10	-.27a	.26	-.01	.15	58

Note: Beta weights are reported. a p<.05, b p<.01, c p<.001, d p<.0001

Table 2.17
Manufacturing Investments, Repression, and Protest

Time Period	ForInv	Amer x ForInv	Afr x ForInv	Asia x ForInv	Repress	Pop	GovExp	R2	N
	-.32a				-.15	-.08	-.33a	.21	58
1967-		.42b			.09	.12	-.34b	.28	58
1969			-.45c		-.14	-.08	-.35b	.32	58
				.07	-.05	.00	-.34a	.14	58
	-.24				-.04	.13	-.26a	.16	58
1970-		.24			.02	.26	-.21	.17	58
1972			-.37b		-.03	.12	-.28a	.24	58
				-.04	-.01	.21	-.24	.11	58
	-.12				-.11	.14	-.17	.10	58
1973-		.39b			.02	.28a	-.12	.21	58
1975			-.33a		-.10	.11	-.19	.18	58
				-.11	-.08	.21	-.16	.09	58
	-.18				-.20	.05	.06	.08	58
1976-		.27			-.11	.17	.13	.11	58
1978			-.38b		-.20	.02	.04	.18	58
				-.21	-.17	.16	.08	.09	58

Note: Beta weights are reported. a p<.05, b p<.01, c p<.001, d p<.0001

CHAPTER SUMMARY

The findings from the analysis in this chapter provide some support for the propositions derived from the arguments of those who maintain that foreign investments are responsible for both absolute and relative deprivation. To the extent that they exist, however, these mechanisms affect only one type of conflict among some types of countries under certain international conditions. Absolute deprivation is prevalent among African countries during the uncertain international circumstances found in the late 1970s. For these countries during this time period, one finds that higher levels of manufacturing investments are associated with lower levels of per capita growth and that this is related to greater amounts of internal war. Apparently, the countries in the world's poorest region suffer tremendously when international economic conditions sour, for not only do their economies slow down, they also find that large scale internal violence increases. From this, one might conclude that absolute deprivation mechanisms require more than mere poverty but must be accompanied by the proper international economic conditions (the problems associated with recessions and other disruptions) and by certain sorts of ties to the international arena (high stocks of foreign investments).

As far as relative deprivation is concerned, one finds both that this mechanism centers on those countries that are somewhat better off and that international prosperity is the sort of soil in which it is most likely to appear. Latin American countries with high stocks of manufacturing investments displayed a tendency toward greater concentrations of incomes in the hands of the wealthy which was related to more internal war during the period of international growth found in the late 1960s. To the degree that international forces such as foreign investment promote concentrated incomes, it appears that the effect is most pronounced among the older and somewhat more developed parts of the Third World. These income disparities only lead to trouble, however, during periods of growth, for it seems that the very poorest members of society tend to resent most the inflated lifestyles of the wealthy when they perceive that they have some prospect for improving their own lot, as was the case during the late 1960s. When economic trouble looms, the poor are forced to focus their attention on scratching out a living and they have less time and energy for violent political action.

This chapter also provides evidence to support the liberal conception of how foreign investments affect domestic conflict. In the first place, the results for flows of foreign investments clearly reveal what seems to be a liberal mechanism, for higher flows in Asia are associated with greater growth throughout the 1970s and this is related to lower amounts of internal war during the 1976–1978 time period. Second, the agricultural findings reveal that stocks of foreign investments in this sector tend to lead to the retention of workers in the agricultural arena that liberals describe. This is associated with fewer political protests, with these effects appearing most strongly in Africa. Finally, stocks of manufacturing investments in Africa were related consistently and directly to less protest.

Based on these results, one can develop some tentative regional profiles. Among the very poor countries of Africa, one finds that foreign investments both increase and decrease domestic conflict, depending on the type of investment and the sort of conflict one examines. Stocks of manufacturing investments are associated by way of an absolute deprivation mechanism with more internal war in the late 1970s. These same investments also are related to a substantial and continuing reduction in the level of political protest. Investments in the agricultural sector appear to be related directly to less turmoil and seem to reduce protest by way of a process in which they help to maintain higher levels of employment for agricultural workers. The evidence indicates that foreign investments are very much a mixed blessing for African states. On the one hand, manufacturing investments appear indirectly to increase the incidence of a very serious and highly destructive form of conflict, internal war. On the other hand, investments in both manufacturing and in agriculture consistently reduce the levels of political protest and, to a lesser extent, turmoil.

In America, foreign investments have a more consistent effect, for when there is an impact on conflict, the tendency is toward increases, rather than decreases, in the level of trouble. The results show that manufacturing investments are related to more internal war by way of a relative deprivation mechanism and that these same investments also are associated with higher levels of protest. Beyond this, investments in agriculture are related to a greater incidence of protest.

Finally, Asian countries appear to be affected less than those in the other regions investigated, for the only relationship found for these states had to do with the liberal tendency for flows to produce more per capita growth, which in turn tended to lead to lower levels of internal war in the late 1970s.

These results suggest that deprivation processes center on one type of conflict, internal war, and occur under very different types of social and international circumstances. Absolute deprivation most affects societies that are newly independent, extremely poor, and that confront the substantial problems that are found during periods of international economic downturns. Relative deprivation, however, has its greatest effects in societies that have been independent for a longer period of time, that are relatively wealthy (by Third World standards), and that are experiencing the benefits that are associated with a time of international expansion.

One might also conclude from the findings in this chapter that foreign investments also produce liberal effects in developing countries. These effects are almost entirely centered in the very poorest and newly independent countries of Africa and tend to greatly affect the incidence of the least violent form of conflict, political protest.

As interesting as these results are, they leave open two basic types of questions. First, one must ask about the way in which certain key social, business, and political segments in developing countries respond to a large foreign presence. Second, one must inquire about the role that nationalism plays in the conflict process. These are the topics that are addressed in Chapters 3 and 4.

NOTES

1. The presentation in this chapter is necessarily brief. For a detailed discussion, the reader should consult Feierabend and Feierabend 1966, Gurr 1968, Lichbach 1989, and Sederberg 1994.

2. Frustration is not always released as aggression and that aggression does not always take on the form of interpersonal conflict. See Lorenz 1966.

3. Even those who use the societal approach employ extensively the concepts and frameworks developed by psychological theorists. There is no clear demarcation between the two approaches. The clearest distinguishing feature between the approaches that have been outlined is found in the research strategies that are employed. Sederberg (1994, 113–129) provides an excellent discussion of this point.

4. The system need not satisfy all of the people's expectations. Deprivation theorists simply argue that the gap between wants and the fulfillment of wants must be kept tolerable, with "tolerable" left undefined.

5. See Johnson 1966 for a discussion of this point.

6. Sederberg (1994) uses the terms decremental and aspirational deprivation when discussing what are referred to here as absolute and relative deprivation. Lichbach (1989) also distinguishes between differing forms of deprivation and provides an excellent discussion of the literature pertaining to relative deprivation.

7. For thorough discussions of Marxist conceptions of the reasons for political conflict, see Tucker 1970 and Boswell and Dixon 1993.

8. Lichbach (1989, 459–461) also discusses the connection between poverty and inequality and how this affects conflict.

9. Muller and Seligson (1987, 428) strongly argue that the income inequality found in Iran was one of the most potent causes of the Shah's downfall.

10. Some scholars regard an inequality in land ownership in itself as the force producing trouble in the agricultural sector. For example, Huntington (1968, 375) writes that "where the conditions of land ownership are equitable and provide a viable living for the peasant, revolution is unlikely. Where they are inequitable and where the peasant lives in poverty and suffering, revolution is likely, if not inevitable."

11. These schools of thought are not entirely uniform. Within any particular set of views there often are differences from one author to another and sometimes even within the body of the works produced by a single author.

12. These labels are from Rothgeb 1989b, 41–49. The presentation here is necessarily brief. A more complete account can be found in Rothgeb 1989b.

13. The authors expressing these views make a distinction between stocks and flows of foreign investment. Stocks are defined as the total value of foreign holdings at any point in time. Flows are the value of new capital that enters a country during a particular period of time. Higher flows are treated as contributing to greater levels of growth because they represent additional capital, which is one of the key ingredients required for growth. Larger stocks, however, supposedly dampen a country's growth prospects because they give foreigners a greater degree of control over local resources (which may be siphoned to locations outside the country) and because they are an indication that the local market is saturated and has less potential for further growth. For a more detailed presentation of these arguments, see Bornschier and Chase-Dunn 1985. For a counter argument, see Rothgeb 1990a.

14. Ayres (1975) expresses similar views.

15. Research by Armstrong (1981), Richardson (1976), and Richardson and Kegley (1980) indicates that there is a general reluctance by poor and subordinate states to accept control by a stronger partner, and Moran (1974), Sklar (1975), and Evans (1979) describe the uneasiness that developing country governments feel as far as the appearance of corporate domination is concerned. Finally, Dolan et al. (1982) describe economic well-being and autonomy as vital to a government's legitimacy, particulary those that rule in the developing world.

16. One of the most important problems confronting those who systematically investigate the effects of inequalities in land ownership on political conflict has to do with the measurement of the independent variable. Prosterman and Riedinger (1987, 25–26) and Brockett (1992, 172) argue that measures of the concentration in land ownership (most notably, the Gini concentration ratio) are flawed for several of the following reasons: (1) they contain little information about the changes that occur in the agricultural sector, (2) they are difficult to calculate with reliability, and (3) they do not measure the degree to which there is a landless population. Other measures,

such as Midlarsky's measure of patterned inequality, also are controversial because of the degree of variation in the calculation of the scores from one society to another (Muller et al. 1989).

17. Midlarsky (1988) argues that another variable, a comparison of the patterns of land ownership between the poorest and the wealthiest members of the agrarian sector, referred to as patterned inequality, is important for gaining a complete understanding of how rural problems contribute to the onset of political conflict. The decision to focus on commercialization and the changing patterns of agricultural employment is not meant to suggest that patterned inequality is not important and plays no role. Instead, it reflects a desire to explore another avenue of inquiry. As noted, there are questions regarding the best means for calculating the measure of patterned inequality (Muller et al. 1989).

18. For a discussion of world systems theory, see Wallerstein 1974 and Bornschier and Chase-Dunn 1985.

19. The author is aware of the various problems Mahler (1980, 5–13) mentions in his excellent discussion of the uses of cross-national designs but agrees that such research provides valuable insight into the relationships investigated. The actual sample for each statistical test is less than eighty-four due to missing data for some countries in the data set. The SPSSX (1983) package was used to conduct the analysis. A "Select If" command was employed to separate out cases for which there were complete data. This procedure is used in the analysis in each chapter of this book. The problem of missing data tends to affect states from all geographic regions of the developing world and therefore should not introduce undue bias into the results. Lists of the specific countries that are included in each statistical test are available from the author upon request.

20. This does not mean that all the relationships followed linear patterns. Instead, it means that no clear nonlinear patterns warranting data transformations were found. Scatterplots depicting the relationships between error terms and independent variables and between predicted values and error terms also were used to assess the problem of biased estimates (Hibbs 1973, 207; Berry and Feldman 1985, 73–76). In no case were any patterns found that indicated that there was a problem.

21. Friedrich (1982) argues that the use of nonsaturated regression equations is unacceptable because one obtains an inadequate picture of the effects of the interaction terms when there are no controls for the main effects of the variables used to create those terms. Allison (1977, 150) disagrees with this view, noting that it is built on the dubious assumption that "additive relationships somehow have priority over multiplicative relationships." Althauser (1971, 465) also disagrees, pointing out that when one uses saturated models plagued by multicollinearity, "the size of the interaction regression coefficient tends . . . to be depressed relative to the coefficients for the individual terms." While some may disagree with their use, nonsaturated regression equations are an acceptable, and perhaps even a preferred, means for assessing multiplicative interaction effects when multicollinearity is a problem. Only the results for the main effects of foreign investment and for the regional interaction terms are reported due to space limitations.

22. The measurement of political conflict for cross-national research has come under close scrutiny in recent years. Brockett (1992, 169–171) points out that the most frequently used data set, *The World Handbook of Political and Social Indicators*

(Taylor and Hudson 1972; Taylor and Jodice 1983), suffers from a tendency to omit important information because it relies heavily on one news source, *The New York Times*, which often does not report events that can be gathered from more regionally oriented news publications. As an example of the problems this can create, Brockett (1992, 170) notes that in the mid-1970s, data collected from regional sources indicated that among Central American countries, Guatemala should have the highest score for violent conflict, followed by Nicaragua, El Salvador, Honduras, and Costa Rica. In the *World Handbook*, however, the ranking for the same period had Honduras as the most violent, followed by El Salvador, Guatemala, Nicaragua, and Costa Rica. These discrepencies lead Brockett to conclude that *World Handbook* data are of questionable value, since he argues that the same problems most likely plague the scores for countries in other parts of the world. Deficiencies of this sort are extremely serious and require careful attention. One of the reasons that COPDAB was used in this analysis is that while COPDAB produces conflict scores that are similar to those that are produced by the more frequently used *World Handbook* data set (see Rothgeb [1991, 21] for an extensive comparison of the two data sets), it avoids some of the problems associated with an overreliance on a single news source. According to Azar (1980, 1982), the COPDAB data set is based on the use of seventy news sources, the vast majority of which are devoted to reporting on each of the world's regions. As a result, COPDAB should be less prone toward the underreporting that Brockett regards as undermining the *World Handbook* data set. One means for examining this is to look at COPDAB's ranking of violence in Central America in the mid-1970s (1973–1975) and to compare it to the ranking developed by Brockett. To do this, each Central American state was ranked according to its score for COPDAB 15 (the point on the COPDAB scale that corresponds to extremely violent domestic conflict, as described below in the text). When this was done, the ranking of countries had Guatemala as the most violent, followed by Nicaragua, El Salvador, Honduras, and Costa Rica. This is the ranking that Brockett argued would be most appropriate for Central America during this time period. As a further check, the COPDAB 15 ranking for the late 1970s (1976–1978) was compared to Brockett's ranking from most to least violent for that period. Brockett suggests that Nicaragua should be first, followed by Guatemala and El Salvador (Brockett does not specify which should be ranked second), Honduras, and Costa Rica. This is the same ranking that one finds when using COPDAB 15. Therefore, based on these results and on the fact that COPDAB makes extensive use of multiple news sources from around the world, it would seem reasonable for one to conclude that COPDAB data may be employed for conducting the types of cross-national tests that are used in this analysis. At the same time, this author realizes that cross-national data sets all have deficiencies, that substantial work must be done to improve their quality, and that the results obtained from using such data should be viewed as tentative.

23. Hardy (1979, 212), Muller (1985b, 51), and Gurr and Lichbach (1986, 6) argue that weighted measures are preferable to raw measures because they better indicate the challenges made to the political system. In this case, the weighting procedure allows one to determine the role of political conflict relative to the stream of other political events in society. It is presumed that when political conflict occurs frequently in comparison to other events, a society is plagued with trouble. It has been brought to the author's attention that the weighing procedure used creates the possibility of

inflated scores for countries with few total events. This problem was investigated carefully. A t-test comparing the average weighted score for each time period for groups of countries with a total number of events falling above and below the mean and the median numbers of total events was used to examine the problem. If inflated scores due to a low total number of events is a problem, then states with fewer events should have significantly higher scores. In no case was this true. It is concluded that the use of weighted scores does not lead to difficulties.

24. Constant 1970 U.S. dollars were used in calculating all monetary values in this book. The sources of the data reported monetary values in U.S. dollars; there was no need to convert local currency. When monetary values were not reported in 1970 U.S. dollars, the deflator for GDP reported by the World Bank (1976, 1980, 1983) was used.

25. In any analysis, many variables must be considered as controls. These variables do not exhaust the possibilities. They were chosen for theoretical reasons and because they often are discussed as affecting the relationship between dependence and conflict. Additional analysis was conducted to determine if using other controls would lead to different results. The other controls included were for foreign and domestic sources of strain (persisting structural sources of trouble) and stress (short-term fluctuations in socioeconomic performance), as Gurr and Lichbach (1986) suggest. Parallel analysis controlled for ethnolinguistic fractionalization (domestic strain), trade as a percentage of GDP (foreign strain), and the change in the terms of trade (foreign stress). Growth in GDP per capita (domestic stress) is included in the results that are reported. In each case, the relationships between foreign investment and political conflict were unaffected by the inclusion of the alternative control variables.

26. GDP was used in preference to gross national product (GNP) because GNP includes "net factor income received from abroad" (World Bank 1976, 6), which contains the income of citizens that is derived from activities in other countries and excludes the income of noncitizens that is remitted abroad. GNP figures partially represent production found in other countries and exclude a portion of the production found in the economy in question. GDP, however, represents the total value of "all goods produced and services rendered within (a state's) territory by residents and nonresidents" (World Bank 1976, 5), and, therefore, is a better representation of the effects of foreign investment on the economic performance of the host state. In order to avoid the potential problems that often accompany the study of growth, percentage real increases in growth were used instead of figures for absolute growth (Jackman 1980).

27. The data used to measure income inequality are from World Bank sources (see Appendix B), as recommended by Mahler (1989). Mahler (1989) and Weede and Tiefenbach (1981, 262) maintain that it is useful to base one's analysis of inequality on more than one measure of inequality. Accordingly, a parallel analysis was conducted that measured inequality as the share of total income for the entire society that goes to the wealthiest 5 percent of the population. In all cases, the results were very similar (except, as expected, for an opposite sign on the regression coefficients) as those that are reported.

28. Among others, Muller (1985b) and Boswell and Dixon (1993) use a measure of repression that is based on the evaluation of a government's respect for civil rights. As mentioned in the text, Hibbs (1973) and Hartman and Hsiao (1988) employ a different operationalization, examining the frequency of government acts that are designed to

suppress and control behavior that the government deems unacceptable. This analysis adheres to the latter approach in the belief that it better taps the concept of repression.

29. The author realizes that some scholars argue that regional analysis is inferior to work that specifies the characteristics that result in differences between political units. As Przeworski and Teune (1970, 8) put it, "The goal of comparative research is to substitute names of variables for the names of political systems." While there is sympathy for this ideal approach here, regional variations are examined in this chapter because previous research shows that this variable retains considerable importance for differentiating between patterns of behavior. Many cultural, political, and international factors vary on a regional basis, and while the aim of research might be the attainment of Przeworski and Teune's goal, for the present the analysis of regions remains a valuable approach.

30. Nie et al. (1975, 381–383) and Lewis-Beck (1980, 54–56) recommend using dummy variables for constructing interaction terms of this sort.

31. The three-year measurement interval was used instead of longer periods to avoid having shorter-term changes masked by lengthy measurement intervals (Muller 1985b).

32. See Rothgeb 1986a for a detailed discussion of how the role of foreign investment changes under differing international economic conditions.

33. Rothgeb (1986a, 134) notes that foreign investment data relating to sectoral location only exist for 1967. One is forced to use these data when examining other time periods. Correlations (using Pearson's r) between figures for total stock of foreign investments indicate, however, that there is a high degree of stability among the data (Rothgeb 1986a, 134). The use of 1967 data was not regarded as unacceptable. Still, the results should be treated as preliminary.

34. Some theorists draw a sharp distinction between the effects of stocks and flows of foreign investments on growth, with flows supposedly leading to higher immediate growth, while stocks are suspected as producing lower levels of longer-term growth (Bornschier et al. 1978; Bornschier and Chase-Dunn 1985; Rothgeb 1989b). As a result, the analysis in Chapter 2 investigates the varying effects of stocks and flows of foreign investments on per capita growth.

35. Studying indirect relationships also involves the analysis of additional equations in which the effects of the independent variable (foreign investment) and the intervening variable (per capita growth, in this case) on the dependent variable (political variable) are examined separately. These results are not presented to conserve space. The relationships between foreign investment and political conflict were unaffected when this intervening variable was omitted from the analysis and the intervening variable had similar effects to those that are reported when it was examined in equations that omitted the foreign investment variables. The unreported relationships from these additional equations were examined for each of the other intervening variables examined in this chapter. Unless otherwise noted, the results for the independent and intervening variables in these additional equations closely mirrored those that are reported.

36. The analysis of the relationship between foreign investment and per capita growth was replicated employing a control for gross domestic fixed capital formation (domestic investment) as a percentage of total GDP. Bornschier et al. 1978, Jackman 1982, and Rothgeb 1989b regard domestic investment as a key control variable when

exploring this relationship. In each case, the reanalysis produced virtually identical results to those that are reported. The reporting in Chapter 2 omits the domestic investment results in order to maintain comparability between the tables.

37. In their analysis of a sample of all independent countries, Weede and Tiefenbach (1981, 274) report a strong relationship between inequality and GDP per capita and GDP per capita squared, which indicates a curvilinear relationship. These authors argue that when these GDP per capita terms are included as controls, there is no relationship between foreign investment and inequality. In order to determine whether such controls would affect the relationship between foreign investment and inequality among the sample of developing countries examined, parallel regression equations were examined that included these GDP per capita terms. In each case, the relationship between foreign investment and inequality was unaffected by the inclusion of the additional control variables. At the same time, GDP per capita and GDP per capita squared were related to inequality in much the same way that Weede and Tiefenbach report.

38. Moore's (1966) classic research on revolutions and social change clearly indicates that agrarian change and land ownership patterns were not the keys to upheavals, but that social and government institutions and interactions were far more responsible.

39. The work of other researchers suggests that a curvilinear relationship exists between repression and political violence such that higher and lower levels of repression are related to lower levels of conflict, and medium levels of repression are related to higher levels of conflict (Muller and Seligson 1987). This possibility was examined carefully by creating dummy variables to represent high, medium, and low levels of conflict. However, the curvilinear relationship described was not found. The explanation for these differing results is probably found in the varying measurement techniques that were employed for operationalizing repression. Muller and Seligson based their measure on the degree to which a government respects civil and human rights. This study employs a measure that is based on the degree to which a government engages actively in behavior that is designed to restrict the activities of those that it regards as its opponents.

CHAPTER 3

FOREIGN INVESTMENT
AND MOBILIZATION

In this chapter attention turns to the second of the three approaches to the analysis of interdependence and political conflict that is mentioned in Chapter 1. This is the mobilization model. The primary differences between the mobilization model and the deprivation approach have to do with the analysis of the question of the motivations that lead to conflict and the roles played by organized groups. As described in Chapter 2, deprivation theorists predominantly focus on the role of denial in the conflict process and on how differing types of denial may lead to an aggressive and violent reaction that not only threatens the stability of the government but endangers the organization of society as a whole. For deprivation theorists, the key considerations pertain to determining what types of social and cultural patterns create the disposition toward violence and how this violence plays out to affect the political community as a whole.

Mobilization theorists analyze conflict from a different point of view. Scholars using this approach pay far more attention to the following three key problems: (1) the role played by groups and organizations in the conflict process; (2) how people are induced to join movements and groups and why they participate in conflict; and (3) how social changes affect groups and motivate them to engage in conflict. While deprivation theorists tend to focus on what makes large numbers of people angry enough that they direct violence toward those who are in authority, mobilization theorists tend to examine the conflict process as a part of a calculated decision on the part of a group and its members to take a particular form of action to secure a desired end product (Lichbach

1989, 462). As Klandermans (1984, 583) puts it, "Mobilization theory emphasizes the importance of structural factors, such as the availability of resources to a collectivity and the position of individuals in social networks, and stresses the rationality of participation in social movements."

The basic premise for mobilization theorists is that organized entities are fundamentally important in most, if not all, conflict situations (Snyder 1978, 505). Given this, one concern for the analyst must be determining why people join organizations and contribute their resources in sufficient amounts so that the group is able to engage in conflict. Beyond this, one also must examine the social conditions that incline groups toward conflict. In considering these conditions, the emphasis is not so much on poverty and other forms of deprivation as it is on circumstances that upset the balance of privileges and political influence in society, thereby creating the need for new social configurations.[1] Among the most cited such changes are those associated with the penetration of a society by foreigners, with foreign investments and trade occupying center stage as particularly influential among the economic elements that can create social instability. Many scholars focus special attention on investments, especially those located in more modern sectors, such as manufacturing, as an important international force for change in developing countries by introducing new values, new production techniques, and new social relationships (Holsti 1975; Rothgeb 1989b, 39–74).

This chapter investigates systematically the degree to which direct foreign investments in manufacturing contributes to domestic political conflict by way of a mobilization process. In doing this, the discussion is divided into three parts. The first provides a brief description of the theoretical arguments presented by mobilization theorists. The second discusses the appropriate means for operationalizing and testing mobilization arguments. Finally, mobilization-based hypotheses are tested to determine the degree to which they are supported by empirical evidence. Before turning to these topics, one point should be noted. This has to do with the fact that many of the arguments presented in this chapter have only recently been introduced into scholarly debate, especially as they relate to foreign investments and other forms of interdependence. As a result, the empirical literature devoted to testing propositions derived from mobilization discussions is sparse, particularly when compared to the deprivation approach.

MOBILIZING FOR CONFLICT

Scholars who take a mobilization approach to the analysis of domestic political conflict concern themselves with the following three broad questions: (1) why people involve themselves in various types of political, social, economic, and other organizations; (2) when, how and why these organizations engage in political conflict; and (3) the factors that contibute to or inhibit the success of these organizations when they do resort to conflict. This chapter builds the conceptual foundation for the later discussion of how foreign investments contribute to mobilization by briefly examining these questions.

Why People Join

At its most basic level, mobilization theory begins with the question of why people are prepared to join organizations and participate in movements. Participation in an organization demands the expenditure of resources such as time and money and often takes an individual away from other enjoyable activities (Mainwaring 1987, 141). In answering this question, mobilization theory treats the decision to join as a part of a rational calculation wherein the individual weighs the expected gains from participation against the possible costs. The individual also is depicted as attempting to estimate the probabilities associated with gains and losses. The decision to join is envisioned as involving a situation in which someone thinks carefully about the following: (1) what she (he) can expect to reap (for example, higher wages, a cleaner environment, or favorable government policies on an issue that is considered important); (2) the probability that the benefit actually will be provided; (3) the (positive) value attached to the benefit; (4) the losses from participation (for example, the inability to engage in recreational activities or the time that might be spent in jail if the group activity strays over the line between legal and illegal activities); (5) the probability that the cost will be incurred; and (6) the (negative) value assigned to the cost (Toch 1965; Lipsky 1968; Olson 1968; Tilly 1978; Klandermans 1984; Oliver 1984; Muller 1985b; Muller and Opp 1986; Mainwaring 1987).

According to this calculus, an individual is most likely to participate when the expected benefits are significant and highly valued, the probability of success is estimated as great, the potential costs are low, and the chance of having to pay those costs is perceived as unlikely (Fireman and Gamson 1979, 33–35; Klandermans 1984, 589). Insignificant benefits or highly valued benefits that one does not believe can be attained substantially reduce the incentives to participate. Likewise, extremely high costs and the perception that it is nearly certain that one will have to pay those costs act as a strong deterrent to participation.

The consideration of why people become involved does not end here, however, for there also is the question of what are referred to as "free riders" (Olson 1968). The free-rider effect is found when the benefits of group activity produce a collective (or public) good, one that all interested members of society are able to consume even if they do not pay the costs associated with the provision of the good. Examples would include wage increases that are the result of union activity but that go to both union and nonunion employees, clean air, and the protection derived from a strong national defense apparatus that go to taxpayers and non-taxpayers alike. When the results of group activity produce goods of this sort, the incentives for individuals to contribute to the attainment of the good tend to evaporate, for each individual is confronted with paying the costs associated with participation in exchange for a benefit that would be available whether they helped to secure the good or not.

As described by Olson (1968), the free-rider effect presents a major theoretical problem for those who analyze any form of collective political action, including political conflict, as a product of a rational calculation because a rational individual naturally would refuse to become involved in collective efforts since such involvement would mean paying costs that could be avoided. Several solutions to this theoretical dilemma are found in the mobilization literature. One revolves around the special incentives, such as legal aid, health care, or an information service, that an organization may provide only to its members (Olson 1968). Another focuses on coercion, wherein those who might be expected to participate but who refuse to do so, such as workers in a plant who do not join a union strike, face the prospect of severe physical punishment, adding a cost to nonparticipation to counterbalance the costs of participation (Gamson 1975, 57). A third centers on soft incentives to participate that are not associated with the provision of the public good, such as an individual's sense of identification with group members, a desire to have fun by working with the group, and the need to belong to a larger organizational entity (Kornhauser 1959, 166; Fireman and Gamson 1979, 21; Klandermans 1984, 591; Oliver 1984, 604; Muller and Opp 1986, 474).[2] Finally, there is the possibility that those who become involved do so because they highly value the good in question and believe that they cannot rely on the efforts of others. As Oliver (1984, 602) notes, "Activists are often quite pessimistic, believing it unlikely that they will be able to rely on the efforts of their neighbors. People who believe others will provide the collective good are motivated to free-ride; people who do not believe others will provide the collective good are motivated to provide the good themselves or do without."

Mobilization theory is based on the notion that an individual's participation in collective action can best be represented as a rational decision that compares the individual's estimates of the costs, the benefits, and the probabilities of having to pay those costs and benefits. While the possibility of free riding clearly exists, mobilization theorists provide several plausible explanations as to why such behavior should not be expected to disrupt completely this decision calculus. As noted, this characterization of how political conflict might occur is very different from the more emotionally based expectations derived from deprivation theory.

Having briefly outlined the individual's incentives to participate, attention now turns to how mobilization theorists depict the activities of organizations.

Organizational Behavior

The analysis of how and why groups mobilize for conflict parallels the discussion of why individuals become involved. The starting point is found in the contention that the goal of all political activity is everyone's desire for more resources (Lasswell 1936).[3] This desire leads to political controversy because all societies have limited resources that are not capable of meeting the sum total of all the demands that are made on those resources. Two methods are available for handling this controversy. The first is to increase rapidly the available resources, allowing the society to meet its internal demands. Examples of efforts of this sort include such things as policies of imperial conquest and the promotion of speedy economic growth. A second, more common, solution is to distribute the available resources in such a manner as to make as many people as possible at least partially happy (Olson 1982, 42). This second approach effectively creates a bargain among the members of society as to the proper allocation of resources.

In striking this bargain, political power and influence is the key to how resources are divided. In other words, some actors will be better able to secure resources than others. This is the point where groups enter the picture, for such organizations have advantages over most individuals in gaining control of resources. This is because groups represent the aggregated demands of many people which provides them not only with a louder voice but with the ability to create the impression that their demands are more legitimate than those presented by others. Organized groups often perform important social functions that allow them to press for a greater share of resources for their members as a means for guaranteeing that they will continue to carry out the function (Gamson 1975, 114; Oberschall 1979, 59; Olson 1982, 37–41). The division of resources in any society reflects the distribution of political power among the varying elements in that society at any given point in time, and one principle purpose of an organized group's activity is to secure as large a share of the available resources as possible for its members.

This bargain, however, is dynamic, for all societies undergo constant change. As change occurs at least three of the following things happen to the balance of power among the groups that determines the distribution of resources: (1) some groups become less powerful in comparison to others, (2) some groups become more powerful when compared to others, and (3) new groups organize to represent the interests of members of society who previously had little or no incentive to organize. These changes in the relative status and number of groups need not lead to political conflict or violence if the following are true: (1) the authoritative decision makers for society recognize the legitimacy of the new groups, give them a place at the bargaining table, and begin the process of introducing reforms to meet their claims; (2) the groups that have lost influence concede a share of their resources gracefully; and (3) the groups that have gained in power do not press unreasonable demands upon the others (Lipsky 1968, 1149; Gamson 1975, 32). If these conditions are not met, the way is paved for conflict.

Tilly (1978, 144–147) notes that the conflict that occurs as groups vie for resources may be placed into two distinct categories. The first is labelled reactive behavior and the second, proactive. Reactive behavior is the sort that is used by those who seek to protect an established position of privilege. Here one finds that organizations "resist changes that would threaten their current realization of their interests . . . [and] they fight . . . against the loss of power" (Tilly 1978, 135). Reactive behavior leads to what is referred to as defensive mobilization (Tilly 1978, 73–74). Mainwaring (1987, 140–141) points out, however, that reactive behavior is not solely a result of the action of a social elite that seeks to protect its positions and interests, for even those who are mired in poverty often join movements and participate politically when they believe that changes are afoot that might endanger such meager resources as they control. Moore (1966) concurs, arguing that a fundamental source of agrarian tension in prerevolutionary France was found in the peasants' perceptions of threats to their modest share of society's resources.

Proactive behavior is found when a group asserts new claims and seeks to take advantage of the new opportunities that it believes are opening up to it as a result of favorable changes in the social and economic climate. Such action produces offensive mobilization (Tilly 1978, 73–74). When the group pressing the new claims is recognized as a legitimate contender for social resources and already possesses a sufficient pool of resources that others feel that they must bargain with it, the proactive behavior may occur as a part of a vigorous bargaining process and may not lead to political conflict. When the group is not so recognized and it does not have such resources, the possibility of conflict increases. Oberschall (1979, 46–47) explains that in the latter circumstance political disturbances serve as the equivilent of the group's resources, providing it with a form of leverage that may be used to trade for concessions on the part of those who control access to the resources that are sought. Those who are not granted the place at the bargaining table are depicted by mobilization scholars as using dissident behavior as a part of a strategy for being taken seriously and provided with what they regard as an appropriate share of the available social resources (Lipsky 1968, 1145; Freeman 1979, 185).

In the case of both reactive and proactive behavior, the resort to political conflict is viewed as a rationally calculated endeavor to secure desired social outcomes. The use of this rational strategy is not automatic, however, for it is conditioned by the cost/benefit analysis that is described in the discussion of individual behavior. A group's cost and benefit calculations center on the value of the good sought, an estimation of the probability that group action will secure the good, the losses the group expects to incur if it acts, and the estimated probability that the group will in fact experience the losses associated with acting.

Several factors are described as affecting the calculations about the probability of receiving benefits.[4] Among the most important of these has to do with communications.[5] The communications process enters into group calculations in several ways. For one, it is central to the groups' awareness of social change, how it is affected, and what it can expect to do about it (Kornhauser 1959, 40; Migdal 1974, 9; Tilly 1978, 7; Olson 1982, 167–168). Without such information, a group is unable to initiate any sort of response.

The key to obtaining this sort of information is found in an efficient and open media and in a population that is sufficiently educated so that it is aware of and understands the implications of social events.

A second type of communications has to do with the ability of the group's leadership to maintain contact and to pass information to the other members of the group. In the absence of this, the group is unable to pull its members together for action when necessary and expectations about the probability of success will fall (Lipsky 1968, 1144; Gamson 1975, 14–16; Tilly 1978, 7; Molotch 1979, 71). Oberschall (1979, 63) notes that such a communications process is most effective when it occurs within the context of the normal social interactions found in a society, such as attending church or going to school or to work, and Olson (1982, 167–168) argues that urbanization also facilitates this type of communication by putting people in close proximity to one another.

A third important part of the communications process relates to the group's ability to get messages to other groups that may act as allies and to those in the general public who may be sympathetic to the group's cause (Gamson 1975, 7; Freeman 1979, 187; Molotch 1979, 71; Griffin 1992, 131). Communicating with interested outsiders increases the group's probability of success by magnifying the pressures on the authoritative decision makers that the group wishes to influence. Such communications may play an important part in determining what type of conflict (protest, turmoil, or internal war) a group may feel compelled to use. As Lipsky (1968, 1151) explains:

The success of protest activity seems directly related to the amount of publicity it receives . . . if protest tactics are not considered significant by the media, or if newspapers and television reporters or editors decide to overlook protest tactics, protest organizations will not succeed. . . . Like the tree falling unheard in the forest, there is no protest unless protest is perceived and projected.

The estimated probability of success for protest declines dramatically when the communications media either is poorly organized or is muzzled by those in authority. In such circumstances, a group most likely will either accept its fate because of its inability to affect change or it will adopt tactics, such as internal war, that are louder and therefore more likely to draw attention to its cause (Gamson 1975, 73).

A final key element to the communications process pertains to the group's ability to interact and bargain with the society's authoritative decision makers. Easy access to those in authority means that groups are not placed in the position of having to engage in extreme forms of conflict in order to get a hearing for their grievances (Gamson 1975, 73). Access may be available either because of a group's strength or because the political system is open. Parvin (1973, 279), Tilly (1978, 152–153), Midlarsky (1988, 492), and Rothgeb (1991, 17) note that stronger groups that can bargain directly with decision makers have little reason to resort to conflict since they already have what conflict usually is designed to obtain: the opportunity to be heard. Such groups often have a basic commitment to society and are wary of engaging in conflict out of a desire to avoid disrupting its basic structures.

When a political system is open and decision makers are easily approached by those with grievances, it has the effect of making the use of force appear illegitimate (Muller and Seligson 1987, 430). Interestingly, while this may reduce the tendency toward violence, an open system may encourage the use of nonviolent protest as a means for exerting pressure on authorities, for the very openness of the political process may promote the belief by would-be protestors that they run few risks but have much to gain from the use of such tactics (Lipsky 1968; Freeman 1979). In this case, the nonviolence of the protest may serve to illustrate how serious a group's grievance is without exposing the group to the charge that it is behaving in an illegitimate manner. At the same time, a harsh reaction by those in authority may be perceived by the members of society as a whole as illegitimate because it is out of proportion to the group's behavior. A government that opens itself up to social contacts and extensive communications often is depicted by scholars as increasing the chance that it will confront some types of conflict (nonviolent protest) while decreasing the probability that it will face others (turmoil and internal war).

As far as the costs associated with political conflict are concerned, one factor stands out: government repression. As mentioned in Chapter 2, repression involves deliberate attempts by the government to restrict or to punish those members of society that criticize or oppose it. When a government is known for the use of such practices, then the costs of conflict generally are regarded as increasing substantially (Gurr 1968, 1120; Hibbs 1973, 113; Tilly 1978, 158; Oberschall 1979, 56; Muller and Seligson 1987, 429). Rothgeb (1991, 19) notes that at least two elements must be included when calculating the costs of repression and the probability that those costs will be paid. The first is the strength of the government. Government strength is important because it increases both the probability that dissidents will be apprehended and the scope of the punishments that can be meted out. Weak governments have a hard time tracking down their opponents, while strong governments not only can catch them but have the resources to devise a wide range of punishments. The second element is the government's reputation for using repression. When a govenment is well known for its repressive policies, the cost estimates for those contemplating political conflict increase due to the knowledge that the probability that they will pay a penalty if caught is substantially higher.

In general, the scholarly analysis of how and why groups mobilize for conflict focuses its attention on conflict as a product of political, social, and economic changes that upset the relative bargaining power of the groups that comprise society and creates the need for a new distribution of resources. One major source of such change results from the penetration of a society by direct foreign investments, particularly those found in modern sectors, such as manufacturing. Conflict is conceptualized as a resource that is traded to obtain influence when one has nothing else to trade, and cost/benefit calculations are the key to whether a group resorts to political conflict. Conflict is not seen as automatic but may be headed off by authoritative decision makers who introduce timely reforms or by a willingness on the part of other organizations to reallocate resources to those who have a claim to a larger share. In this case, the group obtains the benefits it seeks without incurring the costs and running the risks of conflict. When this does not occur, the probability of conflict increases. Certain types of social conditions are envisioned as facilitating, or easing, the onset of conflict.[6] Among the most important of these are the following: (1) a well-developed communications system, (2) an educated population, (3) urbanization, (4) the political influence of the affected groups, and (5) the openness of the political system and government. Elements that dampen the likelihood of conflict are those that increase the cost, such as government strength and the tendency for the government to use repression against its opponents.

Interdependence and Competition

If social change is the source of political conflict as mobilization theorists say, then it is only natural that attention should center on the international system as the origin of some of the most important of these changes. As Gourevitch (1978) points out, scholars have for some time regarded such international events as wars, arms races, and imperialism as major determinants of domestic change and of the political processes and structures found within the nation–state actors in the international system. In recent years, the virtual explosion of international commerce that has been seen since the end of World War II has brought with it the recognition that these quickly expanding economic linkages also might lead both to domestic change and to conflict.

A general picture has been presented of the mechanisms that some scholars believe can translate social change into conflict and how foreign investments can contribute to that process. Now, another more specific conception of the relationship between the changes resulting from international commerce and the onset of political conflict is introduced. The emphasis is on the degree to which these linkages shift the balance of forces in society to the advantage of some and the disadvantage of others, creating winners and losers by opening some new opportunities while at the same time foreclosing others.

The most thorough presentation of the arguments examined is found in Rogowski's (1987, 1989) work. Rogowski discusses the relationship between international trade and domestic instability. Referring to the Stolper-Samuelson Theorem, it is argued that increased international contacts benefit those who use factors of production that the society has in abundance and that are used efficiently by world standards. At the same time, such linkages harm groups that use factors that are scarce and that are used inefficiently (Rogowski 1987, 1121–1122). A society that is poor in capital and rich in labor may be used as an example. In this case, increased international contacts would introduce more abundant and efficient foreign capital, threatening local capitalists with destruction at the hands of their foreign competitors. Labor, however, would benefit because its ready availability and lower cost (due to its efficiency) would put it in a good position relative to its international competitors, leading to more jobs and to higher wages.

When international interdependence leads to advantages for some and disadvantages for others, the potential for conflict increases, for those who gain may be expected to engage in proactive behavior as they pursue a greater share of society's resources, while those who lose may react by seeking to avoid having to pay the full costs of competition. Rogowski (1989, 16–20) argues that two factors conditioning the degree to which conflict actually breaks out have to do with whether the government institutes reforms that are sufficient to placate the winners or enacts policies that are designed to protect or compensate the losers. If such action is taken, then the probability of conflict diminishes. If not, the chance of trouble increases. Whether the government agrees to reforms or protection depends in turn on the strength of the actors involved. Strong labor organizations and powerful business associations should have the government's ear. Weaker and less important actors, however, may be forced to turn to political conflict in order to compel the government to take them seriously and to trade the desired policies for the cessation of conflict.

Many developing countries exhibit precisely the characteristics described. The capitalist class in these countries usually is weak in comparison to its international counterparts and either is confronted with the need to compete with international behemoths that have substantial advantages as far as technology, entrepreneurial talent, and capital availability are concerned (Reuber 1973, 78–91; Vernon 1977, 93; Moran 1978, 90; Frank 1980, 60–61), or is faced with the prospect of acting as suppliers, local contractors, and distributors for much larger foreign enterprises (Reuber 1973, 91; Richardson 1978, 36–38). In either case, the outcome is bound to be unsatisfactory. Operating as adjuncts to foreign firms rarely is acceptable as a permanent condition (Frieden 1981, 416), and those who must go up against multinationals in a head-on contest face the specter of ruin. As a result, capital is inclined toward demands that it be shielded from foreigners and that multinationals have restrictions placed on their activities. Olson (1982, 168) observes that in such a situation local businesses "have an obvious interest in protection against imports and discriminatory legislation against the foreign or multinational firms with which they compete."

The desire on the part of local capital in developing countries for protection does not automatically lead to conflict, however, because local firms often play an important part as allies and supporters of the regime. Evans (1979), Collier

(1979), Duvall and Freeman (1981, 1983), and O'Donnell (1988) are among the many scholars who describe the prominent role of domestic business people in helping to build the coalition supporting many developing country governments. Gold (1988, 191) explains that local entrepreneurs frequently are essential to the government's well-being because they provide employment in a society where jobs usually are needed, they are a vital source of foreign exchange, and they are a major force in the government's programs for economic development. Under such circumstances, local business leaders have such a degree of special influence with the government that they have no need to engage in political demonstrations in order to have their voices heard.

Deyo (1987, 194) and Frieden (1987, 184) report that when local capitalists do not enjoy such clout with the government, things may be very different and political disturbances do occur. Gereffi (1978) describes the political trouble and protests brought on in Mexico when foreign drug companies attempted to shoulder aside Mexican firms, and Kaufman (1979) discusses similar occurrences in Argentina, Brazil, and Mexico when small local firms in petrochemicals, steel, and auto parts faced the onslaught of stiff competition from multinational firms.

As far as labor is concerned, a large foreign presence, either by way of trade or through investments, often leads to benefits for workers because of increased employment at higher wages, especially in the manufacturing sector (Reuber 1973, 167–174; Frank 1980, 75–76). These economic benefits frequently lead to heightened political expectations among those who work for multinational enterprises of the sort that result in proactive behavior (Bollen 1983, 469; Kowalewski 1987, 520). Mainwaring (1987) reports that this political activity often is not confined to those who are employed by foreign firms but may be copied by those who work for domestic manufacturers and who feel that they should have the same benefits and privileges as their fellow workers who are in foreign employ.

Whether political action does in fact break out, however, is a product of three of the following factors: (1) the degree of worker organization, (2) the introduction of reforms, and (3) repression by the government. Each of these factors has been described as important to the onset of conflict. Considerable past research indicates that while they do exist in many developing countries and that they frequently are politically oriented, working class groups tend to be poorly organized and underfinanced (Ananaba 1979; Berg-Schlosser 1982; Chazan 1982; Spalding 1977; Winckler 1988). Some scholars discuss developing country governments as short-circuiting labor unrest either by distributing sufficient political and material benefits to workers that they feel no need to take action (Deyo 1987; Spalding 1977; Winckler 1988), or by employing a degree of repression that acts as a sufficient deterrent to such behavior (Kowalewski 1987).

Rogowski's views suggest that the interdependence resulting from a large foreign presence in the manufacturing sector should lead to conflict on the part of certain very specific groups. One group includes the many petite entrepreneurs who either are forced to go head-to-head with foreign manufacturers who make goods or provide services that compete directly with those that are provided by much smaller local firms or who must be prepared to operate as appendages of the substantially larger multinationals, accepting a position of permanent inferiority or subservience. Members of this group are expected to engage in defensive mobilization in reaction to the foreign presence that is designed to protect them from undue foreign competition and domination.

A second group is composed of those members of the working class who directly benefit from foreign penetration by working for multinational manufacturers at higher wages. Such workers are projected as prone toward conflict because of their desire to translate economic advances into political and social opportunities of the sort that might previously have been denied to them. Locally employed manufacturing workers may also be inclined toward conflict in an effort to obtain similar pay and benefits. According to the general mobilization model presented in this chapter, such worker activity should be most prevalent in societies with a highly unionized workforce. Considerable research by scholars concerned with organized labor in developing countries casts doubt on this, however, by indicating that labor organizations in poorer societies often are in no position to play this role.

SUMMARY OF MOBILIZATION

Mobilization-based presentations regarding the onset of domestic conflict stress the importance of the dynamics between key groups in society and how conflict may erupt when those dynamics are altered by fundamental social changes, with forces originating in the international arena serving as one important source of such change. In general, change is described as most likely to lead to conflict in urban societies that have an educated population, a free press, an open government, a well-developed communications infrastructure, and a government that does not resort to excessive repression but is slow to enact meaningful reforms that address the issues created by change. One also finds in the literature a more precise picture of some specific types of groups that should be most affected by a foreign corporate presence in the manufacturing sector. These groups include local businesses that are hard pressed by foreign competition or that exist only as foreign satellites and members of the working class who are employed by foreign firms or who aspire to acquire the same levels of pay and other benefits that are enjoyed by such employees.

Before turning to the empirical analysis, a word is in order about the nature of the conflict that one might expect from these mechanisms. Considering the types of provocations that have been described and the groups that supposedly are involved, one might hypothesize that mobilization-based conflict will center on political protests. This expectation rests on the arguments of Parvin (1973, 279), Tilly (1978, 152), and Midlarsky (1988, 492), who state that violence is instigated by those who have no stake in preserving the basic organization of society. In the case of interdependence-induced mobilization, conflict is seen as a response to socioeconomic change by groups that do have a stake in society and that only seek adjustments to suit their special interests. Randall and Theobald (1985, 141) note that higher wages and other benefits of the sort that accompany foreign investments create a degree of conservatism in the working class, and Frieden (1987, 184) discusses the fundamental commitment that local capitalists feel for the system even as they protest the role of foreign investment. Zimmermann (1983, 182) maintains that socioeconomic change of the sort that has been discussed as leading to mobilization "cannot be considered to be an important direct determinant of political violence." The expectation is that the mobilization processes under consideration will be associated with political protest.

These projections are analyzed empirically in this chapter.

THE RESEARCH DESIGN

The same basic cross-national research design employed in Chapter 2 is used here to investigate the degree to which the mobilization mechanisms described affect the relationship between foreign manufacturing investments and political protest, political turmoil, and internal war. The focus on manufacturing investments is a product of the many claims in the international political economy literature that these investments are more responsible than are other types of investments for the sort of fundamental political, social, and economic changes that unleash mobilization processes. Investments in this sector often are described as producing either threatening challenges for local businesses or as reducing at least some of these enterprises to a satellite status, and they are depicted as creating new opportunities for the local labor force by paying higher wages and distributing better employment benefits than usually are available from domestic employers. As a result, one might argue that examining these investments provides an excellent test of mobilization claims, for if any form of foreign activity in a host society might be expected to produce mobilization-type activity, it would be direct investments in the manufacturing sector. At the same time, if these investments do not display these sorts of effects, then one must doubt the validity of the arguments discussed in this chapter.

As is the case in Chapter 2, multiple regression analysis is used to examine the hypothesized relationships. Checks were made for outliers by examining Cook's D, scatterplots of the bivariate associations between the independent and dependent variables were examined to determine whether nonlinear patterns existed, and the independent and control variables were regressed on one another to see if multicollinearity was a problem. Scatterplots depicting the relationships between error terms and independent variables and between predicted values and error terms were used to assess the problem of biased estimates. The only methodological problem to emerge from these tests had to do with the multicollinearity that existed when one examined the effects of multiplicative interaction terms with the use of saturated regression equations. This problem was solved much as it was in Chapter 2, with separate equations used to investigate the interation terms and the main effects of the variables that were employed to create those terms.

The mobilization arguments described suggest that cost/benefit calculations are a key to the decision to engage in political conflict. These arguments indicate the need to include a very specific set of control variables in the analysis. In particular, most scholars who focus on mobilization argue that one must control for the degree to which actors might expect to pay costs when they resort to conflict (Gurr 1968; Hibbs 1973; Muller and Seligson 1987; Rothgeb 1991). As mentioned in this chapter, two variables are important for the analysis of costs. They are as follows: (1) the strength of the government, and (2) the degree to which it engages in acts of repression. With one exception (described later in this chapter), each of these variables was included in the regression equations examined in this chapter. The size of the host country also was controlled for. These variables were measured as they were in Chapter 2.

One of the primary differences between the deprivation arguments in Chapter 2 and the mobilization projections in this chapter has to do with expectations regarding causal mechanisms. In the deprivation discussion, the basic claim was that foreign investments were responsible for creating certain types of social patterns in which some members of society were at a distinct disadvantage when compared to others. In other words, foreign investments were described as causing the deprivation that produces conflict. The mobilization presentation pursues a different approach, arguing that a large foreign presence interacts with certain types of social characteristics to produce conflict. Mobilization theorists claim that while foreign investments produce change, this change only leads to conflict when certain sorts of social conditions are present. By extension, the absence of these circumstances would mean no conflict. Mobilization theorists do not, however, hold foreign investments responsible for the creation of the basic conditions that must be present before change produces conflict. Therefore, the proper analysis of mobilization contentions should center on the interaction between foreign investment and certain key social characteristics of the host society and how this interaction is related to political conflict.

The necessary interaction effects were examined by using multiplicative interaction terms that were constructed in a manner that was similar to the procedures employed in Chapter 2 for the investigation of differing regions of the developing world. The greatest difference between the creation of the regional terms and of the terms employed in analyzing mobilization had to do with the types of interactive variables examined. The regional variables in

Chapter 2 were nominal and were easily transformed into the dummy variables that were required to create the interaction terms.[7]

In this chapter, only one of the variables examined, whether a country has a democratic government, is nominal.[8] The previously used practice only could be applied to that variable. All other variables were either ordinal or interval. As a result, the creation of dummy variables followed a procedure wherein countries were rated as having either a high or low value for any particular variable. The cut-off point used for differentiating between high and low values was the median value for each variable. All countries that had a value for the variable in question that was above the median were treated as having a high value for that variable and were assigned a value of 1 for the relevant dummy variable. Those countries that had a value below the median were regarded as having a low value and were assigned a value of 0 for the dummy variable. These dummy variables then were multiplied by each state's level of direct foreign investment in manufacturing to create the appropriate interaction terms.[9]

The specific variables that were examined for their interaction with foreign manufacturing investments included the following: (1) a society's degree of urbanization, (2) the level of education among its population, (3) its communications capabilities, (4) whether it has a free press, (5) whether it is a democracy, (6) the size and strength of the local business community, (7) the size and organizational strength of its labor force, and (8) whether its government is prone toward the use of repression or toward the bestowal of reforms. Urbanization was measured as the percentage of a country's total population living in urban areas as they are defined by the World Bank.[10] Education was measured as the percentage of a country's secondary school age population that actually attends school.[11] Communications was measured as the average number of radios owned by every 1,000 members of the population.[12]

Freedom of the press was operationalized using Gastil's civil rights index, where countries are rated on a seven-point scale according to the degree of civil liberty allowed by the government to the people. On this scale a value of 1 is given to countries with the greatest degree of civil liberty and a value of 7 is given to those with the least (Gastil 1973).[13] The use of these scores was deemed a particularly appropriate measure for freedom of the press because Gastil's civil rights index employs the degree to which the news media is permitted to engage in the unfettered expression of ideas and information as a basic determinant of the score a country receives on this scale.

Measuring the size and strength of the business community and of the labor force was a challenge because direct measures of the organizational attributes of these groups were not available. Fortunately, acceptable surrogates could be obtained. The size of the business community was operationalized as the percentage of GDP in manufacturing, while the index of business strength was measured as manufacturing as a percentage of total exports.[14] It was assumed that an increasing share of GDP from manufacturing would tend to go hand-in-hand with a higher total number of entrepreneurs in this sector. It was presumed also that the strength of the business community is greater as more of the country's exports come from the manufacturing sector because this is an indication that the society's manufactured goods are competitive enough that they can secure a place in world markets. High sales abroad mean that the manufacturing sector is a source of the sort of international income that should stand representatives from this sector in good stead with the government.

The size of the local labor force was measured as the percentage of the labor force in industry. Strength was operationalized as organized labor as a percentage of total labor.[15] The use of this indicator for size was based on the sort of logic described earlier. Employing organized labor as an indicator for strength assumes that when there are more workers in unions, the voice of the workforce is amplified substantially.

The COPDAB data set was used to measure repression and reform. The repression measure that was described in Chapter 2 was employed for the analysis in this chapter. Reform was operationalized by using values 1, 2, and 3 on the COPDAB scale, which represent government programs, such as creating health clinics for the poor, enacting social security legislation, initiating agrarian reform, and improving the distribution of income among the people. As was true of the other variables measured with COPDAB data, the number of events that were coded as a 1, 2, or 3 was divided by the total events of all types for each of the four time periods.

Multiple regression analysis was used to examine the hypothesized relationships. The regression equations took two basic forms, depending on whether the interaction term was based on the examination of how foreign investments interact with repression. When the repression interaction was investigated, the control for repression was omitted from the equation, yielding the following expression:[16]

$$\text{PolCon} = a + b1 \text{ Repress x ForInv} + b2 \text{ GovExp} + b3 \text{ Pop} + e$$

In all other cases, repression was included as a control variable, resulting in the following general equation:

$$\text{PolCon} = a + b1 \text{ Dummy x ForInv} + b2 \text{ Repress} + b3 \text{ GovExp} + b4 \text{ Pop} + e$$

It should be noted that the term "dummy" is used generically in the above equation to refer to the various terms that were used to examine each of the interactive effects described. It also should be understood that the main effects of foreign investment are not reported in this chapter because they are reported in Chapter 2. The results for the main effects of the variables that are conceptualized as interacting with foreign investment are not reported because they are not the primary focus of theoretical concern.

Having described the research design and the measurement procedures, we can turn to the results for this chapter.

RESULTS

The first set of results pertains to how the interaction between a society's communications capabilities, its level of urbanization, and its foreign investments in manufacturing are related to political protest, political turmoil, and internal war. Mobilization theorists argue that when confronted with the sort of change that accompanies foreign investments, urbanized societies with more developed communications facilities are more likely to experience political conflict because the people of these societies will be more aware of the change and how it affects them (because of better mass communications) and more easily organized for political action (as a result of urbanization). It also is expected that the resulting conflict will take the form of political protest, as opposed to turmoil or internal war.

The findings for communications and urbanization are in Table 3.1. These results strongly support the arguments presented. There is a consistent positive association across all time periods between the interaction term for urbanization and foreign investment and political protest, signifying that more urbanized societies with higher levels of foreign manufacturing investments have greater levels of political protest. Similar findings appear for the communications interaction term. Only in the 1970–1972 time period does one find any contradictory evidence. It also should be noted that neither the communications nor the urbanization terms are related either to turmoil or internal war. The only exception to this appears in 1976–1978 when the communications term is negatively related to internal war. These results may be regarded as substantiating at least a portion of the overall mobilization arguments.

The next set of results relates to the relationship between political conflict and the interaction between foreign manufacturing investments and the degree to which a society has a free press and a democratic form of government. The argument here is that a free press plays a key role in the mobilization process by providing people with accurate information both about the changes that result from foreign penetration and about how some political actors are organizing and reacting to those changes. A free press complements a well-developed communications infrastructure, for the latter provides people with the ability to receive information, while the former will insure that the information is as accurate and complete as possible. As far as democracy is concerned, the expectation is that open governments will experience more political conflict than will closed governments because open governments not only encourage citizen participation but also are far less likely to heap substantial penalties upon those who engage in conflict, particularly if the conflict stays within the bounds of accepted political behavior by remaining nonviolent, as is true of political protest.

Table 3.1
Interaction of Manufacturing Investments and Communications and Urbanization

Time Period	Com x ForInv	Urb x ForInv	Repress	GovExp	Pop	R2	N
			Protest				
1967–1969	.38b		.14	-.46c	.07	.25	62
		.43c	-.13	-.34b	.02	.29	57
1970–1972	.25		.05	-.30a	.11	.13	62
		.34b	-.01	-.24	.24	.21	57
1973–1975	.52d		-.11	-.26	.25	.31	61
		.26a	-.14	-.23	.23	.19	57
1976–1978	.39b		-.04	.06	.30a	.21	62
		.27	.00	.00	.23	.11	57
			Turmoil				
1967–1969	-.13		-.02	-.13	.15	.08	62
		.07	-.05	-.14	.13	.05	57
1970–1972	.21		-.14	.06	-.01	.08	62
		.07	.10	-.12	.00	.03	57
1973–1975	.01		-.12	-.03	.11	.03	61
		.07	-.16	-.12	.09	.05	57
1976–1978	.20		-.24	-.01	.44c	.23	62
		-.09	-.23	-.10	.33a	.18	57
			Internal War				
1967–1969	.08		.11	-.19	-.07	.04	62
		.21	.00	-.17	-.12	.08	57
1970–1972	-.25		.00	.17	-.18	.09	62
		-.13	-.04	.14	-.21	.08	57
1973–1975	-.07		-.11	.18	-.10	.05	61
		-.24	-.10	.20	-.18	.13	57
1976–1978	-.27a		-.11	-.06	-.10	.08	62
		-.04	-.07	-.09	-.12	.02	57

Note: Beta weights are reported. a p<.05, b p<.01, c p<.001, d p<.0001

Table 3.2 has the results for freedom of the press and democracy. The findings show that a freer press interacts with higher levels of manufacturing investments to produce more political protest in all time periods. This conforms to the expectations just mentioned. The democracy interaction term, however, only is related to more protest in 1973–1975 and 1976–1978. There is no relationship in 1967–1969 and 1970–1972. This pattern suggests that higher

Table 3.2
Interaction of Manufacturing Investments and Democracy and a Free Press

Time Period	Dem x ForInv	Press x ForInv	Repress	GovExp	Pop	R2	N
Protest							
1967–1969	-.14		.01	-.35a	-.03	.14	62
		-.36b	.00	-.36b	-.04	.23	62
1970–1972	-.02		.04	-.25	.06	.07	62
		-.26a	.02	-.27a	.02	.14	62
1973–1975	.31a		-.10	-.19	.22	.16	61
		-.32a	-.11	-.17	.10	.18	61
1976–1978	.40b		-.01	.08	.31a	.21	62
		-.27a	-.10	.11	.19	.15	62
Turmoil							
1967–1969	-.27		-.10	-.15	.10	.12	62
		-.07	-.01	-.17	.16	.07	62
1970–1972	.12		-.13	.12	-.01	.05	62
		-.27a	-.17	.08	-.09	.11	62
1973–1975	.07		-.11	-.09	.12	.03	61
		-.01	-.12	-.03	.11	.03	61
1976–1978	.31a		-.20	-.02	.45c	.27	62
		-.08	-.27a	.01	.39b	.20	62
Internal War							
1967–1969	-.05		.08	-.17	-.10	.03	62
		-.08	.08	-.17	-.10	.04	62
1970–1972	-.16		-.03	.10	-.18	.06	62
		-.02	.01	.12	-.13	.03	62
1973–1975	.08		-.09	.16	-.07	.05	61
		.04	-.10	.17	-.08	.05	61
1976–1978	-.24		-.12	-.07	-.11	.07	62
		.08	-.07	-.10	-.05	.02	62

Note: Beta weights are reported. a $p<.05$, b $p<.01$, c $p<.001$, d $p<.0001$

levels of foreign investments in manufacturing only spur political protests in democracies when the society faces the sorts of international economic challenges that were found in the mid- to late 1970's. During earlier periods when the international environment was calmer and more expansionary, there was no apparent tendency for the changes associated with higher amounts of manufacturing investments to interact with a democratic form of government to produce more protest. It should be noted that with two exceptions, the results in Table 3.2 indicate that there is no association between the freedom of the press and democracy interaction terms and either turmoil or internal war. The exceptions are the modest positive relationship between turmoil and the democracy term in 1976–1978 and the weak negative association between the freedom of the press term and turmoil in 1970–1972.

The next set of results are for the effects of the interaction between manufacturing investments and education and government acts of reform on political conflict. The basic arguments here are that an educated population is better able to understand the implications of the changes that are unleashed by foreign investments and to organize in response to those changes, which should lead to a greater tendency toward conflict. At the same time, it is presumed that government sponsored reforms will act to "take the wind out of the sails" of those who might consider engaging in conflict by providing them with at least some of what they might otherwise have felt compelled to use conflict to obtain. Again, it is hypothesized that the most affected type of conflict will be political protest.

The results for education and reform are in Table 3.3. As far as education is concerned, one finds a consistent positive relationship between the education and foreign investment interaction term and political protest, indicating that societies that have better educated populations and higher levels of foreign investments also experience more protest, as was expected. The results for reform present a different picture. Here one finds a negative effect that appears in 1967–1969 and 1973–1975, but fades during the other time periods. The reasons for these differences are not immediately apparent, especially when one considers that 1967–1969 was a period of international prosperity, while 1973–1975 was one of stagnation. In any case, the effect for reform is relatively weak, which forces one to conclude that this variable has only a modest effect at best. These results provide strong support for the hypothesis regarding the effects of education but only weak and intermittent support for the one relating to government reform.

As far as internal war and turmoil are concerned, one finds a continuation of the patterns from the previous tables. Neither interaction is related to internal war, and the only effects on turmoil are both weak and sporadic.

The next results are for the interaction between repression and manufacturing investments. The hypothesis is that when a government has a reputation for the use of repression, there will be a tendency toward less political conflict, even when substantial social change is underway, because of a general fear on the part of would-be participants of the costs associated with action. Table 3.4 has the findings relating to this hypothesis. As can quickly be seen, there is no support whatever for these arguments. The repression interaction term is not related to any form of political conflict during any of the time periods examined. Apparently, those who might be moved toward conflict by the change resulting from international interdependence are undeterred by considerations pertaining to government repression. These results

Table 3.3
Interaction of Manufacturing Investments and Education and Reform

Time Period	Educ x ForInv	Reform x ForInv	Repress	GovExp	Pop	R2	N
			Protest				
1967–1969	.39b		.16	-.43c	.07	.26	62
		-.31a	-.11	-.34b	-.02	.22	58
1970–1972	.30a		.06	-.29a	.11	.16	62
		-.22	.02	-.22	.16	.16	58
1973–1975	.52d		-.07	-.21	.24a	.32	61
		-.26a	-.11	-.18	.15	.15	58
1976–1978	.45c		-.05	.09	.31a	.26	62
		-.19	-.20	.06	.05	.08	58
			Turmoil				
1967–1969	-.07		-.01	-.15	.16	.07	62
		-.06	-.06	-.16	.13	.06	58
1970–1972	.29a		-.13	.07	.00	.12	62
		-.23	-.13	.13	-.11	.09	58
1973–1975	-.03		-.12	-.02	.10	.03	61
		-.12	-.13	-.07	.04	.04	58
1976–1978	.32b		-.23	-.01	.45c	.29	62
		-.31a	-.34a	-.05	.20	.23	58
			Internal War				
1967–1969	.03		.10	-.18	-.08	.03	62
		-.12	.02	-.19	-.14	.05	58
1970–1972	-.21		-.01	.14	-.16	.08	62
		-.06	.01	.11	-.19	.05	58
1973–1975	-.03		-.11	.17	-.09	.05	61
		-.07	-.11	.16	-.14	.06	58
1976–1978	-.20		-.09	-.08	-.09	.05	62
		-.17	-.08	-.13	-.15	.04	58

Note: Beta weights are reported. a p<.05, b p<.01, c p<.001, d p<.0001

lend credence to the arguments of those, such as Chazan (1982, 181) and Aya (1984, 328), who maintain that repression actually does little to stop conflict, and that its only actual effect is to force those with grievances either to alter tactics, to change their base of operations to a more secure location, or to modify other elements of the approach they take as they continue their use of political conflict to oppose governments and policies that they abhor.

Table 3.4
Interaction of Manufacturing Investments and Repression

Time Period	Repress x ForInv	GovExp	Pop	R2	N
		Protest			
1967-69	-.11	-.34a	.01	.14	58
1970-72	-.20	-.24	.20	.16	58
1973-75	-.21	-.17	.15	.12	58
1976-78	-.17	.10	.09	.05	58
		Turmoil			
1967-69	-.04	-.16	.14	.06	58
1970-72	-.23	.10	-.08	.07	58
1973-75	-.02	-.07	.06	.01	58
1976-78	-.02	.05	.27a	.07	58
		Internal War			
1967-69	.04	-.18	-.12	.04	58
1970-72	.13	.10	-.18	.07	58
1973-75	-.01	.16	-.12	.05	58
1976-78	.00	-.10	-.11	.02	58

Note: Beta weights are reported. a $p<.05$, b $p<.01$, c $p<.001$, d $p<.0001$

The size and strength of a country's labor force were considered next. In this case, the argument is that foreign manufacturing investments will tend to produce conflicts in societies with a large and well-organized labor force. The reason for this has to do with the fact that foreign manufacturing corporations tend to pay better wages and to provide more benefits than local firms, which is hypothesized as leading to trouble as laborers take political action to demand more political rights and to seek an extension to locally employed workers of the benefits and wages provided by foreign firms.

The results that are relevant to these expectations are in Table 3.5. These findings reveal that the interaction term for the size of the industrial labor force has a consistent positive relationship with political protest. This variable is positively related to turmoil in 1970–1972 and negatively related to internal war in 1970–1972 and 1976–1978. The interaction term for the organizational strength of the labor force, however, generally is not related to any form of conflict. The

Table 3.5
Interaction of Manufacturing Investments and Labor Force in Industry and Organized Labor

Time Period	LabInd x ForInv	OrgLab x ForInv	Repress	GovExp	Pop	R2	N
			Protest				
1967–1969	.34b		.12	-.43b	.07	.22	62
		-.06	-.06	-.45b	-.04	.23	48
1970–1972	.29a		.03	-.30a	.12	.15	62
		-.12	.03	-.30a	-.01	.11	48
1973–1975	.47c		-.07	-.23	.25a	.28	61
		.25	-.09	-.21	.14	.13	47
1976–1978	.41b		-.06	.05	.31a	.23	61
		.13	-.08	.08	.24	.07	48
			Turmoil				
1967–1969	-.03		.00	-.16	.16	.06	62
		-.16	-.10	-.09	.15	.09	48
1970–1972	.30a		-.16	.06	.01	.12	62
		.11	-.23	.08	-.15	.11	48
1973–1975	-.11		-.13	-.01	.08	.04	61
		-.15	-.23	-.08	.04	.07	47
1976–1978	.16		-.25a	-.01	.43c	.22	61
		-.12	-.37a	-.02	.25	.14	48
			Internal War				
1967–1969	.02		.10	-.18	-.08	.03	62
		-.09	.03	-.22	-.11	.06	48
1970–1972	-.30a		.01	.17	-.19	.12	62
		-.15	-.17	.04	-.30	.13	48
1973–1975	.01		-.10	.17	-.08	.05	61
		-.10	-.19	.25	-.25	.16	47
1976–1978	-.28a		-.12	-.08	-.09	.09	61
		-.46b	-.21	-.19	-.31a	.23	48

Note: Beta weights are reported. a p<.05, b p<.01, c p<.001, d p<.0001

only exception is the negative impact on internal war in 1976–1978. Based on these results, one may conclude that there is strong evidence to suggest that the absolute size of the industrial labor force is associated with some form of proactive behavior that consistently leads to protest. At the same time, the proactive behavior associated with a large labor force clearly is not related to the higher levels of structural violence that are found in internal wars. In fact, there is reason to believe that this variable actually has an inhibiting effect on this type of violence. These results indicate that the organizational characteristics of the labor force have little to do with the incidence of conflict.[17]

The final set of results pertains to the size and strength of the local entrepreneurial community. The hypotheses in this case suggest that, on the one hand, when local manufacturers constitute a strong force on the local scene (with strength being indicated by the ability to export, which not only earns precious foreign exchange, but also indicates the ability to compete head-to-head in the international arena), they either will have little fear of foreign competition or they will have such bargaining power with the government that they will be able to get whatever they want without stirring up political conflict. On the other hand, the sheer size of the local manufacturing community (as represented by manufacturing as a percentage of total GDP) is taken as an indicator of the degree to which there is a class of small entrepreneurs who may be forced either to compete on unequal terms with foreign firms or to operate as adjuncts of foreign corporations, something that it is expected will be associated with higher levels of political protest.

The results for these variables are in Table 3.6. One finds here that the interaction for the size of the entrepreneurial class is positively associated with protest in every time period except 1973–1975. The interaction term representing the strength of the entrepreneurial class, however, only is postively related to protest in 1973–1975 and 1976–1978. Neither variable is related to internal war and the only results for turmoil are the positive associations for size in 1970–1972 and 1976–1978 and for strength in 1976–1978.

The associations between the size and strength of the local manufacturing sector and political protest present an interesting picture. Size appears to be associated with protest during periods of international prosperity (1967–1969 and 1970–1972) and mild recovery (1976–1978), while strength is related to protest during periods of international stagnation (1973–1975) and recovery (1976–1978). This suggests that small manufacturers are most prone to take political action when they are most pressured by their foreign competitors, as during those times of international prosperity when foreign firms are most active. For their part, more competitive local firms seem to behave in a similar fashion, except that for these firms the moments of greatest concern come when a sluggish international situation leaves them unable to compete as effectively as they might in the international arena, which in turn leaves them more exposed to the foreign firms that have invaded their home turf. The result is the tendency toward protest designed to obtain the government's assistance. These conclusions are tentative and additional research is required to test them carefully in other contexts.

Before turning to the conclusions, a word about the control variables is in order. Among these variables, the most consistent results are the negative relationships between government expenditures and protest in 1967–1969 and

Table 3.6
Interaction of Manufacturing Investments and GDP in Manufacturing and Exports in Manufacturing

Time Period	GDPMan x ForInv	ExpMan x ForInv	Repress	GovExp	Pop	R2	N
			Protest				
1967–	.33b		.03	-.34b	.04	.22	62
1969		.10	.08	-.36b	.02	.13	61
1970–	.27a		.01	-.26a	.08	.14	62
1972		.04	.02	-.27a	.07	.08	61
1973–	.05		-.14	-.14	.16	.08	61
1975		.37b	-.20	-.11	.20	.21	58
1976–	.43c		-.06	.13	.27a	.26	62
1978		.40b	-.14	.12	.26a	.23	59
			Turmoil				
1967–	-.01		.01	-.17	.17	.06	62
1969		-.03	.00	-.20	.17	.08	61
1970–	.34b		-.19	.10	-.01	.16	62
1972		.13	-.19	.06	-.01	.06	61
1973–	.17		-.12	.00	.13	.06	61
1975		.14	-.14	-.01	.13	.05	58
1976–	.26a		-.24a	.02	.42c	.26	62
1978		.26a	-.29a	-.01	.41b	.26	59
			Internal War				
1967–	.22		.07	-.16	-.07	.08	62
1969		.04	.10	-.19	-.07	.04	61
1970–	-.04		.01	.12	-.13	.04	62
1972		-.17	.00	.12	-.16	.06	61
1973–	-.05		-.10	.16	-.09	.05	61
1975		.06	-.09	-.02	-.13	.03	58
1976–	.04		-.06	-.10	-.06	.01	62
1978		.09	-.06	-.18	-.12	.05	59

Note: Beta weights are reported. a p<.05, b p<.01, c p<.001, d p<.0001

1970–1972, which indicate that during these periods stronger governments were in a better position to hold down conflict. The precise means that they use for doing this, however, remains an open question that must be addressed in another research context. Another consistent relationship is the positive association between a state's population and its levels of protest and turmoil in 1976–1978. Larger countries appear to have experienced higher levels of both of these forms of conflict during the late 1970s. As has been noted previously, repression does not seem to have a consistent effect on any of the types of conflict examined in this analysis.

CHAPTER SUMMARY

The results from this chapter support the general hypothesis suggesting that direct foreign investments in the manufacturing sector produce social changes that interact with certain types of society and government characteristics to produce political conflict in developing countries. The support for this hypothesis, however, pertains to one type of conflict—political protest—and varies somewhat according to the type of society and government variable one examines.

The strongest and most consistent relationships are found when one considers the interaction between foreign investment and such social characteristics as a country's degree of urbanization, its communications capabilities, the existence of a free press, the educational achievements of the population, the numbers of people employed in industry, and the degree to which manufacturing accounts for a large share of GDP. Additional results indicate that two other variables—whether a country has a democratic form of government and has the ability to export manufactured goods—may play an important role in inducing conflict during international recessions. Specific types of government behavior, such as the use of repression and the granting of reforms, however, either do not interact with foreign investments to produce conflict, or only display relatively weak and intermittent effects. The same is true when one considers the impact of the labor force's degree of organization.

These results point to some important conclusions. The first is that the types of variables that are most likely to facilitate the unleashing of mobilization-induced conflict are those that relate to the following two sorts of social conditions: (1) the ease with which information can flow from person to person within a society and people are able to establish contacts with one another; and (2) the degree to which there are large numbers of people who feel that they are affected by the foreign presence. The rapid communication of accurate information to an educated and urbanized population appears to interact most strongly with a large foreign manufacturing presence to produce political conflict. One also finds evidence indicating both that a large industrial labor force and that a sizable class of small entrepreneurs who must work in the shadow of foreign corporations can be key factors leading to conflict. All of these sorts of social forces appear to create the impetus toward conflict on a constant basis, even when one controls for such things as the government's strength and its use of repression and the types of international conditions that prevail at any particular point in time. The most important forces in the mobilization process, at least as far as foreign investments are concerned, have to do with the ability to communicate and maintain contact and with the existence of a felt need on the part of certain important parts of society that either proactive or reactive behavior is called for.

The results from this chapter also support the conclusion that mobilization processes generally are associated with protest and rarely lead to violence. In other words, those who feel compelled to take action apparently do so within the context of the current political system, seeking changes in policy or in the composition of the government but not the destruction of the system itself. This indicates that the mobilization effects of foreign investment most greatly affect those who have a stake in the current structure of society and who would be loath to take any action that would threaten that structure. The owners of smaller-scale businesses and the more privileged members of the working class fit into this picture.

A final conclusion has to do with the way in which even the strongest and presumably most secure members of society react to a large foreign presence. Among the most important of those who might be included in this category would be entrepreneurs and workers associated with corporations that export goods in large volume. As mentioned in this chapter, many authors argue that the members of this group have such strong influence with the government and such close ties to foreign corporations that together these three elements form what Evans (1979) refers to as a "triple alliance." Given their position of strength and influence, one would, at first glance, expect that the members of this group would be immune to any temptation toward social protest. The results from this chapter suggest otherwise, indicating that when international markets sour, there may be a tendency to turn on other members of the alliance and to use (or to encourage) political protest as a means for pressuring the government to take action to protect home corporations from foreign behemoths. Further research should consider the exact mechanisms that are at work in these situations and precisely who is actively involved in the political activity.

This chapter investigates the degree to which foreign investments are associated with mobilization processes. The results indicate that such effects do occur and that they center on political protest.

NOTES

1. See Moore (1966, 97) for a discussion of how social change unleashes forces that lead to major social upheavals. Kornhauser (1959) and Olson (1963) also discuss the vital role that economic and social change can play in creating political conflict, and O'Donnell (1988, 24) describes the changes resulting from the expansion of the political arena to include new organized actors as one of the most important of the factors that produce conflict in developing societies.

2. In each of these cases, the additional incentive is treated as the equivelent of adding another benefit to the individual's cost/benefit calculations.

3. Resources are broadly defined as anything that a group values and that it is prepared to take action to secure. This may include material objects, public policies, or some form of symbolic recognition.

4. A discussion of the value that the group attaches to the benefit sought is omitted because of the extremely subjective nature of that calculation.

5. In addition to communications, analysts discuss group leadership, group size, the size of the society in which the group operates, and the group's resource base as factors affecting the group's estimate of its probability of success (for example, see Lipsky 1968; Tilly 1978, 7; Olson 1982, 33).

6. Gurr (1968, 1106) refers to these social conditions as facilitators.

7. Regional interaction terms are not included in the analysis in this chapter because creating such terms would involve setting up triple interactions between foreign investment, the mobilization characteristic under examination, and the region in which a country is located. When this procedure was followed in preliminary analysis, however, the result often produced interaction terms with such a low n that the term was not suitable for use in regression analysis. Therefore, the decision was made to focus on the interaction between foreign investments and the mobilization variables that are investigated in this chapter.

8. The coding of a country as democratic or nondemocratic was done by the author. A country was judged as democratic when it allowed an organized opposition to exist and to compete in free and fair elections for control of both the executive and legislative branches of the central government. Each country in the data set was coded for each of the four three-year time periods investigated. In a few cases, a country shifted from democratic to nondemocratic or vice versa during one of the time periods. When this happened, the country was coded as having the type of government that it had for over one-half of the period in question. The sources used to obtain the information for the coding included Arthur Banks, *Political Handbook of the World*, and *The New York Times Index*. In order to check for the consistency of the results that were obtained from the use of these scores, parallel analysis was conducted employing Gastil's political rights index (Taylor and Jodice 1983, 58–61) as a measure for democracy. In all cases, the results conformed closely to those that are reported.

9. In addition to conducting analysis that employed interaction terms that were based on dummy variables that were created through the use of the median, parallel analysis examined the results that would be obtained if another cut-off point was used to construct the dummy variables. This additional analysis was designed to insure that the reported results would not be sensitive to the manner in which the dummy variable was created. States were rated as having a high value if their score for a variable was in the upper quartile of all scores. In each case, the results from the parallel analysis were very similar to those that are reported.

10. The urbanization data from the World Bank covered the years 1965, 1970, and 1975. The figures for 1965 were used for examining the 1967–1969 period, the 1970 figures were used for 1970–1972 and 1973–1975, and the 1975 figures were used for 1976–1978.

11. The secondary school data only were available from the World Bank for 1970. To determine whether the use of these data produced unusual results, additional analysis was conducted that measured a society's level of education by looking at its education expenditures per capita. In each case, the results from the additional analysis were nearly identical to those that are reported.

12. Radio ownership data only were available from the World Bank for 1970. This measure was used because radios represent a widely used form of communications in countries that are poor and that have low literacy rates, as is often the case in the developing world.

13. The civil rights scores were obtained from Taylor and Jodice (1983). This source provides an average score for the years 1973–1979. Scores for earlier years were not available. Yearly scores also were not reported. It should be noted that Taylor and Jodice do report the maximum shift in each country's score during the 1973–1979 period. For the most part, these shifts were extremely minor and were not such that they would lead to a change in a country's position as far as the computation of the dummy variable for freedom of the press is concerned. While the data available were far from ideal, they were judged as providing a reasonable indicator of the concept that was measured.

14. Data for manufacturing as a percentage of total GDP and manufacturing as a percentage of exports were available for 1967, 1970, 1973, and 1976. It is recognized that these data do not separate the activities of domestic firms from those of foreign corporations. Measures that do this are not available. Despite this flaw, these data provide a reasonable indicator of the size and strength of the local business community.

15. Data for organized labor as a percentage of total labor were available only for 1975. Data for the percentage of the labor force in industry only were available for 1965, 1970, and 1975. The figures for 1965 were used for examining the 1967–1969 period, the 1970 figures were used for 1970–1972 and 1973–1975, and the 1975 figures were used for 1976–1978. It was recognized that the figures for organized labor provide only a rough approximation of labor strength in light of the submissive role that unions in developing countries often play (Ananaba 1979; Koo 1987; Spalding 1977). Given the absence of viable alternatives, these data were employed nonetheless. The results are tentative.

16. Omitting the control for repression was necessary to avoid the problem of multicollinearity.

17. The results for the interaction term for the organizational strength of labor may be a product of the quality of the available data. The data employed to measure this variable related to the percentage of workers in organized unions. These unions are in some cases, however, sponsored by the government and therefore may not be useful agents for organizing political action.

CHAPTER 4

FOREIGN INVESTMENT AND NATIONALIST CONFLICT

This chapter examines the degree to which foreign investments produce domestic political conflict by stirring up nationalist reactions in the host society that lead to a xenophobic backlash against multinational corporations. In doing this, the analysis focuses on a problem that is very different from the processes that have been investigated in earlier chapters. In those chapters, attention centered on the role that international dependence and interdependence might play in producing winners and losers in the host society either by creating political, social, and economic structures and processes that would benefit some members of society at the expense of others (the deprivation model) or by spurring fundamental social and economic changes that would incline people to band together for proactive or reactive political action (the mobilization model). This chapter takes another approach, exploring the possibility that a large foreign presence might be associated with such a specter of foreign domination and an accompanying loss of local autonomy that members of the host society are induced to engage in acts of political conflict.

In considering this possibility, three different mechanisms are examined. The first treats nationalist backlashes as a product of rapid social changes that undermine the traditional values of a society and that appear to substitute foreign ways of doing things for those traditional values. The second regards nationalist reactions as stemming from the fear that economic dependence represents a new form of imperialism that is designed to subjugate the host society and to render it helpless in the face of foreign exploitation. The third concentrates on the degree to which foreign investors who locate in a society that is divided along ethnic and national lines might be perceived by members of these different subcommunities as aiding one group at the expense of others, thereby fanning the flames of national animosity and jealousy. While these processes are distinctly different, they share one common element, for they all are built on the presumption that the influx of foreigners that comes with extensive international contacts interacts with certain specific characteristics of the host society to create xenophobic conflict.

The logic of these projected connections between international dependence and nationalism is outlined briefly in this chapter. Following this, the same cross-national research design that was used in earlier chapters is employed to test the empirical validity of those assertations. Before examining these subjects, it should be noted that many of the contentions discussed in this chapter have only recently become the subject of scholarly concern as they apply to international interdependence in general and to foreign investments in particular. The literature devoted to the systematic analysis of the propositions that are examined in this chapter is meager.

SOCIAL CHANGE, NATIONALISM, AND FOREIGN INVESTMENT

The first of the nationalist models explored in this chapter is concerned with the interaction between a high level of foreign penetration and rapid social changes in the host society. The focus on social change in this context differs fundamentally from the treatment that it has received in earlier chapters because attention centers on the degree to which change leads to conflict by way of a xenophobic reaction that attributes fundamental alterations in the makeup of society to the machinations of foreigners. Under such conditions, those who are affected by change not only are depicted as having to struggle with new circumstances and the many problems that they create but are described as burdened by the perception that their struggles have been brought on by outsiders who wish to transform society by introducing new and incomprehensible values and ways of doing things.

The starting point for analyzing how change interacts with foreign investment to produce antiforeign outbursts is to consider the arguments of those who see sudden and sweeping social change as the key to conflict. For those who favor this approach, massive changes in social reality are regarded as responsible for conflict because they bring into question the basic belief systems that guide a community and that all members of a society have been socialized to accept as valid and beyond challenge (Toch 1965, 43–44; Johnson 1966, 91). In less-developed societies, urbanization and industrialization often are described as two major forces that are responsible for disturbances of the sort that lead to conflict. As Kornhauser (1959) notes, "The rapid influx of large numbers of people into newly developing urban areas invites mass movements, [and when] industry is introduced [it] involves marked discontinuities in social organization." Weiner (1960, 174) agrees, pointing out that "large numbers of rootless, crowded, and often unmarried urban workers are easily provoked to violence."

According to Migdal (1974, 196–197), urbanization and industrialization create the potential for instability in developing societies by drawing people away from their traditional reference points, which tend to be rural and agrarian, and placing them in new and unfamiliar situations where the rules for proper social behavior not only are very different but may not be easily understood. Once they are removed from their villages and are confronted with laboring in an industrial environment that requires that they live according to rules with which they have had little experience, people become susceptible to extreme behavior. As Toch (1965, 128) observes, people "will tend to become disillusioned if [they] become directly involved in life situations for which [they have] been ill-prepared by socialization." In such circumstances, the political system moves toward disequilibrium because "[traditional] values no longer provide an acceptable symbolic definition and explanation of existance" (Johnson 1966, 72–73). People begin to feel estranged from the community, which can lead to "social atomization [which] engenders strong feelings of alienation and anxiety, and . . . the disposition to engage in extreme behavior to escape from these tensions" (Kornhauser 1959, 32). Huntington (1968, 36–37) sums the situation up very well, writing that when urbanization and industrialization occur,

Social and economic changes necessarily disrupt traditional social and political groupings and undermine loyalty to traditional authorities . . . tendencies toward distrust and hostility . . . are intensified . . . new values undermine the old basis of association and authority . . . [this] breakup of traditional institutions may lead to psychological disintegration and anomie.

The thesis that rapid urbanization and industrialization are associated with greater levels of political conflict is far from universally accepted. Even some of those who present arguments suggesting the possibility of such a linkage often express second thoughts. For example, Huntington (1968, 279–280) maintains that while there are many reasons to believe that rural to urban migration might lead to conflict, there also is a logic suggesting that such a linkage does not exist because newly arriving urban dwellers tend to be overwhelmingly interested in obtaining the basic necessities of life, they are poorly organized, and they have very low levels of political awareness. Each of these factors works strongly against any involvement in political activity. Cornelius (1969, 833–857), Migdal (1974, 117–118), and Berg-Schlosser (1982, 401–405) offer the same sort of observations regarding the behavior of urban-dwelling former peasants in Latin America, Asia, and Africa. Beyond this, Hibbs (1973, 37–39) and Zimmermann (1980, 178–184) point out that in general the evidence from such systematic cross-national research as has been done reveals virtually no relationship between the rates of urbanization and industrialization and the incidence of domestic political conflict. While some authors have constructed a logic implying that one might expect a positive relationship between certain types of social change and political conflict, research indicates that the linkage is at best tenuous.

This is not the end of the story, however, for several scholars argue that the relationship between social change and conflict is too simplistic and fails to account for vital additional elements, the most important of which is the role of foreigners. Johnson (1962, 1–2) asserts that social transformations achieve their potency for producing conflict and violence when they occur in tandem with a substantial degree of foreign penetration, pointing to the example of China in the early twentieth century, where social changes interacted with the growing presence of foreigners to create the conditions that spawned conflict. Skocpol (1979, 50) concurs, arguing that late-eighteenth-century France, and Russia in the first decades of the twentieth century, are additional cases in which fundamental changes in society were reinforced by the growing role of foreigners to create a climate that led to trouble.

Two basic types of processes usually are described as connecting foreign penetration with social change to create conflict. In the first, foreigners become a convenient symbol that can be used as a rallying cry and that can be blamed for the many discomforts that are associated with the transformation of society. Griffin (1992, 147) discusses the importance of using such symbols as a means for focusing the discontent of those who are adversely affected, and Johnson (1962, 69) and Rubin (1981, 266) describe how the political conflict leading to the revolutions in China and Iran was affected by the skillful use of these sorts of symbols to promote xenophobic reactions that helped to undermine prerevolutionary governments that were depicted as little more than the stooges of foreign interests.

A second and closely related process is found when people come to see foreigners as pushing for change in an attempt to subvert and extinguish local customs. As Holsti (1982, 11) notes, "To many . . . people, integration and interdependence imply cultural dilution and possibly extinction." According to this line of thought, the challenges to long-held and deeply cherished value systems that accompany urbanization and industrialization in themselves are not the reason for trouble. Instead, problems only emerge when people come to believe that the new ways of doing things and the new social relationships are part of an attempt by outsiders to undermine local culture and to replace it with an imported, unfamiliar, and unwanted set of beliefs. One important foreign agent that often is blamed for these changes is the multinational corporation. As Rothgeb (1987, 233) writes, these foreign firms frequently are "regarded [by local residents] as introducing foreign values into the host society, thus undermining local culture and creating a host of social problems." Frank (1980, 28–29) and Vernon (1977, 14–15) agree.

Adding weight to these fears is the tendency in such circumstances "for the society to fracture into polarized . . . groups as some members of the system begin to accept . . . [the foreign] alternatives to the old value structure" (Johnson 1966, 80). This division in society reinforces the already high levels of tension associated with rapid change, as traditionalists come to resent the influence and foreign ties of those that they believe wish to undermine the basic essence of society, while more progressive elements deride the traditionalists as out-of-step with social reality and as unable to accept the alternatives that are needed in order to create a better society. When these perceptions regarding the relationship between change and the role of foreigners become deeply embedded and widely held, the probability of conflict is greatly increased, as conservatives seek to protect the values and way of life that they prize so highly from destruction at the hands of foreigners and their domestic allies within the affected society.

One finds a number of scholars who argue that the social transformations that are associated with rapid urbanization and industrialization interact with the penetration of society by foreigners to create political conflict and violence.

IMPERIALISM AND NATIONALIST BACKLASHES

The second nationalist model of conflict is built around the idea that international dependence often is perceived as a part of a pattern of imperialism by which stronger members of the international system attempt to dominate and exploit those who are smaller, less developed, and weaker. Boswell and Dixon (1990, 540) argue that these perceptions often lead to xenophobic backlashes and point to the trouble found in Cuba, Iran, Nicaragua, El Salvador, Philippines, and South Korea as examples of occasions on which nationalist reactions of this sort led to violence. Dix (1983, 289) concurs, noting that the nationalist reactions to the presence of foreigners that accompanies dependence can be an especially potent source of conflict in developing societies.

Rothgeb (1987, 232) explains that in order to understand the connection between international dependence and xenophobic conflict, one must begin by considering the intractable and frustrating problems that plague developing societies. Among other things, the people in such countries confront a dearth of jobs, poor housing, inadequate health care and educational services, an often ramshackle food distribution system, a rapidly expanding population, skyrocketing prices due to uncontrollable inflation, and a stagnant economy that offers little prospect for any improvement in the near future. Under such conditions, it is natural for people to seek a target to blame for their plight, particularly when all of the best efforts of the government, of local business leaders, and of individual citizens to improve things lead only to meager results.

One logical target for blame is foreigners, especially those who are associated with multinational corporations. There are many reasons for this. One is that foreign firms represent a system of commerce (capitalism) that is alien to many developing countries and that is associated with the excesses of the imperial era when so many developing societies were held as colonies (Frank 1980, 28–29). Another is "The speculation that multinational enterprise based in the United States [or in any other advanced home country] is simply an extension of American culture and political interests abroad" (Wells 1971, 98), which leads to the belief that foreign firms are agents that are devoted to dominating and taking advantage of the host society.

A third reason why foreign investors are targets of blame has to do with the tremendous strength that these corporations appear to have when compared to local firms and to the host government. These firms not only have great financial assets, but they possess technology, managerial talent, and access to international marketing and distribution systems, all of which are in short supply in developing countries and are necessary for promoting economic growth and development. Such a disparity in resources lends credibility to the notion that foreign corporations are in some way responsible for the problems of poor countries, either because they have helped to create those problems through exploitation or because they have failed to use their capabilities to try to alieviate the misery that they find in the developing world. Rothgeb (1987, 232) sums up the situation as follows:

Within developing countries, multinational corporations often are the focus of considerable frustration and hostility and are credible targets for blame. Their foreign origins make them suspect. In fact, [many people] frequently perceive foreign investors as actual or potential agents of their home governments. This perception [creates] a skeptical, and often hostile, view of corporate activities.

Spalding (1977, 243–244) notes that this animosity often spills over from the corporation to the local government, creating a general air of resentment toward those who are in authority. Many scholars agree with this assessment of the situation.[1]

While there is widespread agreement in the literature regarding the connection between foreign investments and xenophobic nationalism, there has been little empirical research that explores this relationship. Work that has been done indicates that foreign investments create the sort of controversy that leads to conflict only under certain circumstances. As far as the present discussion is concerned, the most important of these conditions are the following: (1) that the investment must be regarded as exploitative and as contributing little to local development efforts, (2) that the investment should stand out as a highly visible example of a foreign presence, (3) that the investors must appear to have close ties to their home countries, (4) that the investments should be overwhelmingly from a single foreign national source, and (5) that there must be a strong belief in the host state that past relations between the host society and the investor's home country have been exploitative (Rothgeb

1986a, 127–128; 1987, 240). The first and second of these conditions help create the impression that foreigners are the reason for local problems, while the other three all contribute to the perception that foreign corporations are agents of a new form of imperialism that is designed not only to exploit but to control the host society, thereby robbing it of its independence and reducing it to a position of complete subservience.

The first three of these conditions are associated with foreign investments in mining and agriculture. Pinelo (1973, 12–13), Vernon (1977, 149), and Mahler (1981, 273) point out that investments in primary products, such as mining and agriculture, often are seen as exploitative because they remove local resources for what appears as meager compensation and because they lead to foreign ownership of tangible parts of the territory that makes up what is perceived as the homeland. According to Tilly (1978, 3), this violates an implicit general rule found in many societies that "residents of a local community [feel they have] a prior right to the resources produced or contained within that community." Resource extraction projects also are highly visible because they tend to concentrate in small enclaves, or company towns, near the site where the extraction takes place. They stand out as islands of relative wealth in a sea of poverty (Frieden 1987, 189; Mahler 1981, 273; Pinelo 1973, 12–13; Sklar 1975, 25; Vernon 1971, 196). Finally, Reuber (1973, 228) reports that primary product enterprises are very closely tied to their parent firms in the home country, and Wells (1971, 107) states that they make little effort to hide their foreign ties.

Many scholars assert that foreign investments in the manufacturing sector are much less likely to produce xenophobic outbursts than are those in primary products. The reasons relate to the three conditions just mentioned. First, such investments generally are perceived locally as contributing to progress and are not as readily regarded as exploitative (Rothgeb 1986a, 128). Second, the managers of such enterprises frequently attempt to disguise their foreign origins in the belief that doing so helps create a better climate for conducting business and enhancing profits (Becker and Sklar 1987, 9). Finally, manufacturing enterprises often are given a greater degree of latitude for maneuvering without interference from parent firms located in the home country (Sklar 1987, 29).

Based on these arguments, one would expect that the sectoral location of foreign investments makes a difference as far as nationalist conflict that is related to imperialism is concerned. While primary product projects might become the source of xenophobic nationalist outbursts, it seems less likely that investments in manufacturing will have a similar effect.

The final two conditions pertaining to when foreign investments produce nationalist conflict relate to whether the investments are from a single foreign national source and to the level of past exploitation in the relationship between the home and host societies. Diaz-Alejandro (1970, 329) argues that when foreign investments are predominantly from a single foreign national source the image of an imperial presence is enhanced because of the tendency among host country citizens to see corporations with a common national origin as working together to control the host society. Lipson (1985, 105) and Rothgeb (1987, 233) make similar points. Galtung (1971) reaches the same conclusion from a different angle, maintaining that a high percentage of investments from a single foreign source creates the impression that one is caught in a feudal pattern of international interactions in which one is totally dominated by just one other member of the international system, leaving one with little ability to pursue one's own best interests.

Past exploitation in the relationship between the host country and the investor's home state are of importance because foreign corporations often are viewed as working hand-in-hand with their home governments to help further the government's policies. If the home government is perceived as domineering and as having taken advantage of the host society, there may be a tendency to transfer such perceptions from the government to the firm and to believe that the firm is attempting to undermine the host state's independence and to pillage the host country.

The belief that a domineering relationship exists is most probable under three conditions. The first is if the bulk of the host state's foreign investments are from the United States. Magdoff (1969, 15) is among the numerous theorists who assert that many in the developing world regard the United States as the central agent of imperialism in the post–World War II world. Simon (1988, 139) makes a slightly different point, noting that the vast economic, political, and military strength of the United States creates a substantial degree of unease in developing countries due to the belief that too close an association with Americans will inevitably result in excessive domination. Taiwan is cited as an example of a country where such perceptions are prevalent.

The second and third conditions pertain to whether the host country is a former colony that only recently has achieved its independence, or if the host society receives the bulk of its foreign investments from the state that once held it in imperial bondage. The people of new states or states that receive most of their foreign investments from the former imperial master are described by many scholars as very likely to perceive such investments as an attempt to continue an informal brand of the formal imperialism that once led to their exploitation (Leslie 1987, 132–133; Rothgeb 1986a, 128; Vengroff 1975, 246). In these societies, foreign domination is an issue that touches a particularly raw nerve, for as Nehru once stated, "We consider colonialism [as] permanent aggression" (quoted in Wilcox 1962, 142). Among the people in these societies "the dominant [concern] . . . in dealing with the rest of the world is their inbred antipathy to the old colonial powers" (Calvocoressi 1962, 36) and all that they regard as associated with them, such as multinational corporations. As a result, the sort of large foreign presence entailed by high levels of foreign investment often is viewed as an unacceptably dangerous inroad on the part of foreigners that threatens local independence. A local government that allows such a presence may be treated as a foreign puppet that must be changed or removed by way of whatever political action is necessary.[2]

Based on these arguments, one might hypothesize that higher levels of foreign investments in primary product sectors (mining and agriculture) will be associated with greater levels of xenophobic nationalist conflict in newly independent societies when the investments predominantly are from a single foreign national source and that source is either a country's former colonial overlord or the United States.

ETHNONATIONAL DIVISIONS AND FOREIGN INVESTMENT

The third process that is hypothesized as connecting foreign investments to nationalist conflict has to do with the way in which a large multinational presence is regarded as interacting with the ethnonational divisions that are found in many countries across the globe.[3] This mechanism differs from the two mechanisms discussed in that in those models, conflict is directed at outsiders and against a government that is perceived as overly tolerant of outsiders either in an attempt to slow or halt unwelcome social change or to eliminate unacceptable foreign domination. Whichever the reason, the focal point of the conflict is foreigners who have established too great a presence in the host society. In the case of ethnonationalist conflict, however, the strife is between different groupings within the host country, with foreign investments serving as a catalyst that helps to force to the surface such ethnonationalist grievances as may exist within the host society.

Connor (1993, 374–375) notes that significant ethnonational divisions are found in the vast majority of the states that make up the international system, and Zimmermann (1983, 204) reports that cleavages of this sort are widely regarded by scholars as associated with domestic conflict. One reason these divisions frequently are described by social scientists as a potent source of domestic trouble is because such cleavages are regarded as hindering the state's ability to establish itself as legitimate and to create a broad sense of loyalty among its people. Rothschild (1981, 14) reflects these sentiments when he writes that "Ethnic nationalism . . . remains the world's major ideological legitimator and delegitimator of states, regimes, and governments. A state's legitimacy depends heavily on the population's perception of the political system as reflecting its ethnic and cultural identity."

Burg and Berbaum (1989, 536) assert that the state's difficulties in establishing its legitimacy are found in the tendency for ethnonationalist divisions to block its efforts to create a single national identity, stating that "Multinationality is widely viewed in the comparative politics literature as an impediment to integration at the mass level and therefore as a threat to political stability." According to this view, the existence of several ethnonational groupings is regarded as a source of conflict because differing peoples simply prefer to be ruled by those from their own group and they have a hard time accepting and according legitimacy to a government that is composed of leaders from other ethnonational segments of society. This problem is magnified as the number of these groups increases because of the greater complexity of the resulting social cleavages and the higher probability of animosity between any two or more ethnonational elements in society.

Another connection between ethnonational cleavages and conflict is based on the notion that such social divisions often are the basis for inequality. According to this line of thought, the "competition [for resources] is the critical process shaping patterns of racial and ethnic relations" (Banton 1983, 12) and "ethnic differences in themselves are neutral realities [as far as conflict is concerned] until they become the basis for ethnic inequality" (Krymkowski and Hall 1990, 322). Deutsch (1979, 69–70) agrees that the political effects of ethnicity and race are greatly enhanced in societies that are highly stratified, and Rothschild (1981, 39) remarks that the "engine of ethnic conflict . . . is the perceived ethnic inequalities and inequities in access to and possession of economic, educational, political, administrative, and social resources."

An uneven distribution of resources among ethnonational groups may take several forms. One is found in a situation in which the ethnonational groups in a state are clustered geographically. Under such circumstances, the naturally occurring variations in the distribution of such things as raw materials, rainfall, soil fertility, and access to the sea may take on political significance by creating pockets of relative wealth and poverty in a country. These uneven distributions of geographical opportunities may serve as the source of strife when advantaged ethnonational groups resist the attempts by central government authorities to use the income from one region to help those who live in other regions. Such a form of resistance is regarded by many social scientists as common because of the tendency for a population to regard as its own the resources located within its geographical sphere. Government efforts to parcel out resources among the state's entire population, as opposed to leaving the resources to the people of a specific region, may serve as the occasion for violence and even for attempts at separation (Horowitz 1981, 167). Wallerstein (1961, 88) refers to precisely this sort of problem when he writes that "Ethnic loyalties can usually find expression in geographical terms. Inevitably, some regions will be richer (less poor) than others, and if the ethnic claim to power combines with relative wealth, then the case for secession is strong." Shaba (Katanga) province in Zaire (Congo) is offered as an example of such a situation.

Regional clustering can have two other effects as well. One is found when educational opportunities are geographically concentrated, allowing some ethnonationalist groups the chance to obtain better training. These groups may then assume dominant positions in the government and in the business community and may be posted to positions in less-favored regions, where they are perceived as carpetbaggers. This may create tensions as the locals, who have other ethnonationalist ties, come to resent foreign dominance. Horowitz (1981, 174–176) offers the Ibo in Nigeria as an example of a favored group that has been the focus of considerable tension, and Wright (1991, 304) describes the Sindhi and Bengali resentment at the control they suffered at the hands of ethnonationalist groups from other parts of Pakistan.

A second source of regionally oriented trouble comes when a region is used as the basis for organizing the government. In this case, ethnonationalist leaders are able to assume very important roles in political decisions, which may encourage them to play up the ethnonationalist distinctions between regions in order to solidify their hold on power. Burg and Berbaum (1989, 538) describe Yugoslavia as displaying these characteristics before it collapsed after the end of the Cold War.

Ethnonationalist distinctions also serve as the basis for inequality when they are the grounds for discrimination in a society. Here one finds that conflict occurs even when ethnonational groups do not cluster in geographic regions. The source of the trouble in this case is found when there is a competition for resources and ethnonational identity is used to determine the degree to which an individual will be permitted a share. The situation is greatly exacerbated when various ethnonational groups regard each other as inferior, when an individual's ethnonational identity is easily determined, and when there is a strong belief that those who control the levers of governmental and commercial authority will act to dispense benefits to fellow ethnonationalists while denying them to others (Deutsch 1979, 54–55; Crighton and MacIver 1991, 139–140).

When these circumstances prevail, Hechter's (1978, 300–301) "cultural division of labor" may evolve. A cultural division of labor exists when differing ethnonationalist groups are accorded opportunity structures and employment patterns that vary dramatically from one another, with some groups receiving marked preferences as far as obtaining more high status and well-paying jobs and social roles, while others are consigned to lower status positions with less influence and compensation. Under such circumstances, some ethnonationalist groups come to dominate the core social positions in society from which public policy is made and enforced, and others are relegated to the periphery, having little, if any, voice in such affairs. As Rothschild (1981, 53) comments, under a cultural division of labor, "cultural [or ethnonationalist] markers . . . distinguish the peripheral and the core populations from each other [and are used for] identifying and categorizing the respective economic roles and functions of these two populations."

When these distinctions between ethnonationalist groups exist, they greatly inflame tensions, for the disadvantaged have a strong incentive to identify with ethnonationalist action groups designed to obtain greater opportunities while those who dominate wish to preserve their status (Hechter 1978, 301). Esman (1987, 397), Brockett (1991, 256), and Wright (1991, 303) describe the existence of these sorts of ethnonationalist interaction patterns in, respectively, Malaysia, Central America, and Pakistan, where native Malays, indigenous Americans, and minority Pakistani ethnic groups have systematically been denied the educational, employment, and property rights granted to other, more favored, ethnonational groups.

Deutsch (1979, 52) and Rothschild (1981, 116) argue that the social, political, and economic tensions between ethnonationalist groups are most likely to flare into confrontations when fundamental social change is underway, and that modernization and growing levels of international commercial linkages are two of the strongest forces that contribute to the change that leads to conflict. As Deutsch (1979, 51) explains, "Modern economic competition, with its heavy premium on social contacts and linguistic skills . . . automatically imposes heavy barriers on all those who do not share the language, experience, and cultural pattern of the locally dominant group." For his part, Rothschild (1981, 4) notes that international linkages have similar effects that favor some ethnonationalist groups over others, stating that

The globalization of science, technology, and economic interdependence is an uneven . . . process, conferring advantages on some regions and groups . . . while relegating other regions and groups to marginality and subordination. . . . These differentiating results of the process contradict its potential egalitarian promise . . . to the extent [that this process] operates within states, these contradictions provoke conflict between advantaged, dominant [ethnonationalist] population segments and disadvantaged subordinate ones.

Nielson (1985, 143) and Krymkowski and Hall (1990, 316) concur, noting that under the conditions that Deutsch and Rothschild describe, ethnonational distinctions often are perceived as the key determinant of who does and does not share in the benefits that accompany modernization and interdependence, thereby creating the possibility of trouble. Hibbs (1973, 76–78) reached much the same conclusion in his cross-national analysis of the relationship between ethnonational divisions and political violence, finding that among societies confronted with rapid socioeconomic change, the probability of political conflict increased in tandem with the number of ethnonationalist divisions.

One of the most potent of the many international forces that promote the sorts of commercial and economic changes described are the direct foreign investments of multinational corporations. As a result, the actions of multinational firms are hypothesized as having the effect of fanning the already smoldering fires of ethnonational disputes (Ihonvbere 1994, 52–54). Foreign investments are seen as doing this in several ways. Multinationals frequently play the leading role in helping to exploit the resources in developing countries. In doing this, these corporations help to increase the disparities in wealth found in differing geographical areas and contribute to the regional tensions described regarding the most appropriate distribution of the proceeds from the sale of natural resources. The activities of Belgian copper companies in Shaba province in Zaire serve as but one example of this process.

Multinational corporations also may exacerbate ethnonationalist problems through their employment and subcontracting practices. For instance, it is not uncommon for foreign firms to employ talented indigenous labor and to do a substantial amount of business with local entrepreneurs (Reuber 1973; Frank 1980). When those who are hired or contracted with either are from an ethnonational group that is not indigenous to the region in question, and are therefore perceived locally as carpetbaggers, or are overwhelmingly from the core or dominant ethnonational group, trouble may brew. In the former case, multinationals may be regarded as aiding and abetting attempts by ethnonationalists from other parts of the country to control the region in question. In the latter, the foreign firm may become a symbol of international support for the prejudicial practices associated with the local cultural division of labor. Indeed, Robinson (1954, 224–225) and Deutsch (1979, 46–47) point out that there often are significant economic advantages as far as the overall costs of labor are concerned when an employer follows discriminatory hiring procedures, a fact that is rarely lost on those who are discriminated against. Again, this can only help to add fuel to an already tense situation.

It is highly likely that multinational corporations that operate in countries that are populated by multiple ethnonational groupings will find themselves enmeshed in the local struggles among these peoples and that their behavior will contribute to heightened levels of conflict. This leads to the hypothesis that higher levels of direct foreign investment interact with a greater variation in a society's ethnonational composition to produce a higher level of domestic conflict.

SUMMARY OF NATIONALIST CONFLICT

In reviewing the literature, one finds three basic models that describe the means by which foreign investment dependence is related to nationalist-based conflict in developing societies. The first regards foreign investments as interacting with the extensive social changes associated with rapid urbanization and industrialization to produce widespread political and social problems in the host country. According to this view, foreign investments in the manufacturing sector are most likely to promote trouble because they bring alien customs, values, and ways of doing business to the host society. It is hypothesized that when this foreign presence is mixed with the unsettling problems that accompany industrialization and urbanization, a potentially explosive situation is created and the result is heightened political conflict, as affected members of the local population lash out at the foreigners and at a government that is too closely associated with them, blaming them for the uncertainties and dislocations introduced by social change. In this case, the conflict is described as violent but disorganized due to the many barriers to close cooperation that exist among people who find themselves in new life situations. Turmoil is the type of conflict that should be most affected.

The second model is built around the idea that the activities of multinational corporations frequently are viewed as a part of a new form of international imperialism that is designed to allow the stronger and wealthier members of the international arena to dominate those that are poorer and weaker. It is expected that such feelings are strongest and most likely to spur domestic conflict when foreign investments are in primary product sectors, such as agriculture and mining, they are located in newer countries, and they are overwhelmingly from a single foreign national source or are from either the United States or from the host state's former imperial master. Primary product investments create resentment because they are perceived as robbing the local population of its natural resource heritage, and investments in new states, from a single source, from the United States, or from a former imperial overlord, are described as creating the impression that a society confronts a foreign effort to use the investments as a means of political control. Imperialist conflict usually is described in the literature as well organized because the dissatisfied are envisioned as having the opportunity to come together to act in concert. This points toward either protest or internal war. There is little indication in the literature as to which of these forms of conflict should predominate; the results from earlier chapters suggest that protest might be most often found because the sorts of grievances that are described as coming from imperialist concerns generally are not the sort of thing that one would expect to lead to the complete disruption of the host state's political and social structures.

The final model treats foreign investments as leading to conflict by interacting with the ethnonational divisions found in the host society. In this case, multinational corporations are depicted as allying themselves, either consciously or unconsciously, with some ethnonational groupings within the host state, fostering both a substantial degree of resentment on the part of those who are not so favored as well as a possible feeling of superiority on the part of those who do benefit from the multinational presence. Those who do not benefit are described as inclined toward conflict out of the desire to obtain a share of the wealth, jobs, and other opportunities that are generated by foreigners, while those who do benefit are depicted as prepared to resist the diversion to others of the economic resources that they believe rightfully belong to their ethnonational group. The expectations derived from this model are not specfic to a sector but are regarded as applying both to primary product and to manufacturing investments. This model projects that the conflict generated will be well organized. Hibbs' (1973, 76–78) research found a positive relationship between ethnonational divisions and political protest. There also is reason to believe that the conflict may be highly violent, as is true of internal war. Examples of such violence are found in the Ibo revolt in Nigeria and the rebellion by Shaba province in Zaire.

All of these models are subjected to empirical analysis in this chapter.

RESEARCH DESIGN

The nationalist models of the association between foreign investment and political protest, turmoil, and internal war are tested here with the same cross-national design employed in earlier chapters. Multiple regression analysis is used to assess the relationships hypothesized by each model. As is the case in earlier chapters, Cook's D was used to check for outliers, scatterplots of the bivariate associations between the independent and dependent variables are examined to determine whether nonlinear patterns existed, and the independent and control variables are regressed on one another to assess the degree to which multicollinearity was a problem. Scatterplots depicting the relationships between error terms and independent variables and between predicted values and error terms also are used to assess the problem of biased estimates.

The only methodological problems were those discussed in earlier chapters. Occasionally, it was necessary to remove outliers from the sample used, and a high level of multicollinearity existed when one examined the effects of multiplicative interaction terms by using saturated regression equations. This problem was solved as it was in earlier chapters, with separate equations used to investigate the interaction terms and the main effects of the variables that were used to create those terms. To conserve space, only the interaction results are reported.

As is the case in Chapter 3, the nationalist arguments presented in this chapter are built around the idea that foreign investments produce conflict by interacting with certain characteristics of the host society. When those characteristics are present, it is projected that conflict will be the result. When those characteristics are not present, there should be a lower probability of a relationship between foreign investment and political conflict. Seven characteristics are hypothesized as a key to conflict. Two are associated with the social change model. These are an increase over time in a country's levels of urbanization or in the proportion of its labor force employed in industry. Four are derived from the imperialist model. They are as follows: (1) the degree to which a high proportion of a country's foreign investments are from a single foreign national source; (2) whether the country is a recently independent member of the international system and may be considered a new state; (3) whether the United States is the single largest foreign national source of a country's foreign investments; and (4) whether a country's former colonial overlord is the single largest foreign national source of its foreign investments. Finally, the ethnonationalist model posits that a society's degree of ethnonationalist diversity will interact with its level of foreign investments.

Analyzing these interactive effects requires, first, that these characteristics be measured and, second, that terms be constructed to represent their interactions with foreign investments in the manufacturing, mining, and agricultural sectors.[4] Measures for the changes in urbanization and in the labor force in industry were based on the data used in Chapter 3 for urbanization and labor in industry, except that in the present context a value representing change was computed by subtracting the value of the relevant variable at the beginning of each time period from its value at the end of the period.[5] The proportion of a country's foreign investment from its single largest foreign national source was measured as the percentage of the total stock of investments that came from all sources. Measuring the United States and colonial overlord variables was based on identifying that single largest source. The data source used to obtain the foreign investment data contained sufficient information to allow for these calculations. Date of independence was used to determine whether a country should be considered new or old. These data were from Banks 1978. Last, ethnonationalist diversity was measured by using a country's ethnolinguistic fractionalization score as reported by Taylor and Hudson (1972).[6] This is a commonly used measure for this variable.[7]

The examination of the hypotheses in this chapter was conducted much as was done in Chapter 3, where multiplicative interaction terms were used. Dummy variables were created to indicate if a particular societal characteristic was present, in which case the dummy was valued at 1, or absent, in which case the dummy was given a value of 0. These dummy variables were then multiplied by the relevant foreign investment variables to create the appropriate interaction terms.

Seven interaction terms were needed. Two of the main effects variables, whether investments are predominantly from the United States or from the ex-colonial master, are nominal and could be created using the procedure for nominal variables that was outlined in Chapters 2 and 3. Another variable, date of independence, was created by assigning a value of 1 to countries that achieved independence after World War II ended in 1945 and a value of 0 to countries that gained independence before 1945. Those countries that received a value of 1 were regarded as new states. The end of World War II generally is recognized as the date when the European empires started to dissolve and the many new states of the postwar era began emerging.[8] The remaining dummy variables for percentage of investments from a single source, for the changes in the levels of urbanization and industrialization, and for ethnonationalist divisions, were created by assigning a 1 to states with a value that exceeded the median value for the sample as a whole and a value of 0 to states with a value that was below the median.[9] Those countries that were scored as a 1 were treated as having a high value for the dummy variable in question.

In conducting this chapter's multiple regression analysis, the same three control variables used in earlier chapters were included: repression, government strength, and the size of the host state's population. These variables were measured as they were in earlier chapters.

The basic regression equations employed in this chapter are the same as those used in earlier chapters, taking the following form:

$$\text{PolCon} = a + b1\ \text{Dummy x ForInv} + b2\ \text{Repress} + b3\ \text{GovExp} + b4\ \text{Pop} + e$$

The term "dummy" is used in the equation to refer to the seven dummy variables described. The main effects of foreign investment are not reported here because they were reported in Chapter 2.[10]

Having discussed the research design and measurement procedures, we may now turn to the results.

RESULTS

The first set of results is for the interaction between a society's degree of change in its level of urbanization and in its labor force in industry and its level of manufacturing investments. Manufacturing investments are conceptualized as most likely to spur the antiforeign nationalist reactions that are supposed to accompany fundamental and rapid social changes.[11] The relevant findings are in Table 4.1. As can be seen, there is little support for these expectations. The rate of urbanization interaction term is not related to any of the measures of conflict during any of the time periods investigated. The labor force change interaction term does not fare much better. This term has a weak positive relationship with protest during 1973–1975 and a modest negative association with internal war in 1970–1972. Otherwise, the results suggest that this variable has no effect on conflict. Based on these findings, one must question the validity of the argument that suggests that a large foreign presence interacts with rapid social change to create conflict.

The second set of results pertains to the interaction terms that represent whether a country's foreign investments are predominantly from the United States or from the former colonial overlord. These results are in Tables 4.2, 4.3, and 4.4. Two things stand out in these tables. The first is that the United States and colonial interaction terms have their greatest effects on political protest, only a small effect on turmoil that varies according to time period, and no effect on internal war. The second is that the manufacturing term is far more strongly and consistently related to protest than are the interaction terms for mining and agriculture. When one consults Table 4.2, one finds that among countries with manufacturing investments that are principally from the United States, there is a consistent and solid positive association between the level of investments and the amount of protest. When foreign manufacturing investments are primarily from the former colonial master, however, one finds a consistent negative relationship with protest. Table 4.2 also reveals that the United States and the former colonial manufacturing interaction terms have few effects on turmoil and internal war. The only significant finding is the negative relationship between the colonial interaction term and turmoil in 1970–1972.

The findings for the United States and colonial mining interaction terms in Table 4.3 are similar to those for the manufacturing term, but less consistent. There is a strong positive relationship for the United States term in 1967–1969 and in 1976–1978 and a negative relationship for the colonial term during the same periods. Both terms also are related to turmoil. The United States term has

Table 4.1
Interaction of Manufacturing Investments and Change in Urbanization and Labor Force in Industry

Time Period	Urban x ForInv	Labor x ForInv	Repress	GovExp	Pop	R2	N
			Protest				
1967–	-.15		-.04	-.31a	.00	.14	57
1969		-.03	-.04	-.32a	.01	.12	57
1970–	-.11		-.01	-.22	.18	.11	57
1972		.05	-.02	-.23	.20	.10	57
1973–	-.12		-.15	-.21	.19	.14	57
1975		.28a	-.13	-.25	.25	.20	57
1976–	-.12		-.09	-.02	.18	.05	57
1978		-.09	-.06	-.01	.19	.05	57
			Turmoil				
1967–	.15		-.03	-.15	.14	.07	57
1969		-.01	-.04	-.13	.13	.04	57
1970–	-.26		.12	-.09	-.03	.08	57
1972		-.02	.10	-.12	-.01	.02	57
1973–	-.14		-.17	-.10	.06	.07	57
1975		-.13	-.16	-.10	.05	.07	57
1976–	.09		-.19	-.09	.35b	.17	57
1978		.19	-.21	-.10	.36b	.20	57
			Internal War				
1967–	.17		.05	-.19	-.11	.06	57
1969		.14	.06	-.18	-.10	.05	57
1970–	.05		-.04	.13	-.19	.07	57
1972		-.30a	-.03	.17	-.25	.15	57
1973–	-.04		-.09	.20	-.15	.07	57
1975		.02	-.09	.19	-.14	.07	57
1976–	.15		-.03	-.09	-.10	.04	57
1978		.04	-.06	-.09	-.11	.02	57

Note: Beta weights are reported. a $p<.05$, b $p<.01$, c $p<.001$, d $p<.0001$

a positive association in 1970–1972, and the colonial term has a negative association in 1970–1972 and 1976–1978. Neither term is related to internal war.

The agricultural findings in Table 4.4 follow much the same pattern as was found for manufacturing and mining investments. The United States term is positively related to protest in 1970–1972, 1973–1975, and 1976–1978, but is not related to either turmoil or internal war. The colonial term is negatively

Table 4.2
Interaction of Manufacturing Investments and the United States and the Colonial Master

Time Period	U.S. x ForInv	Colonial x ForInv	Repress	GovExp	Pop	R2	N
			Protest				
1967–1969	.45c		.18	-.33a	.09	.28	57
		-.41b	-.04	-.32a	-.05	.27	57
1970–1972	.38b		.01	-.20	.13	.20	57
		-.39b	-.06	-.25	-.02	.21	57
1973–1975	.45b		-.01	-.16	.26	.27	56
		-.30a	-.14	-.21	.11	.19	56
1976–1978	.46c		.09	.10	.43c	.31	57
		-.37b	-.03	.02	.30a	.25	57
			Turmoil				
1967–1969	.09		.07	-.16	.23	.09	57
		-.19	.01	-.15	.19	.12	57
1970–1972	.25		.04	-.08	.03	.07	57
		-.39b	-.02	-.11	-.08	.16	57
1973–1975	-.14		-.18	-.09	.07	.06	56
		.05	-.14	-.08	.11	.04	56
1976–1978	.21		-.16	-.03	.44c	.22	57
		-.08	-.21	-.07	.40b	.18	57
			Internal War				
1967–1969	.24		.19	-.16	-.01	.08	57
		-.13	.09	-.16	-.08	.05	57
1970–1972	-.05		-.01	.14	-.13	.04	57
		-.03	-.01	.14	-.13	.04	57
1973–1975	.07		-.06	.21	-.05	.06	56
		-.04	-.08	.20	-.08	.06	56
1976–1978	-.08		-.10	-.10	-.08	.02	57
		-.03	-.09	-.09	-.07	.02	57

Note: Beta weights are reported. a p<.05, b p<.01, c p<.001, d p<.0001

associated with protest in 1970–1972 and in 1976–1978 and displays no relationship with turmoil or internal war except for a modest positive effect in 1973–1975.

On the basis of these findings, it would appear that while foreign investments from the United States are perceived in the host state as a potential source of foreign domination, those that come from the former colonial overlord are

Table 4.3
Interaction of Mining Investments and the United States and the Colonial Master

Time Period	U.S. x ForInv	Colonial x ForInv	Repress	GovExp	Pop	R2	N
			Protest				
1967–1969	.48c		.11	-.32a	.11	.32	53
		-.36a	.04	-.11	-.04	.13	53
1970–1972	.12		.06	-.25	.06	.09	53
		-.22	.07	-.27	-.01	.12	53
1973–1975	.25		-.11	-.19	.20	.16	52
		-.13	-.09	-.22	.11	.11	52
1976–1978	.55d		.03	.11	.49c	.39	53
		-.27a	.03	.04	.29a	.19	53
			Turmoil				
1967–1969	.11		.08	-.15	.26	.10	53
		-.20	.10	-.17	.20	.13	53
1970–1972	.39b		.12	-.10	.05	.17	53
		-.37b	.13	-.16	-.13	.16	53
1973–1975	.11		-.09	-.07	.11	.04	52
		-.14	-.04	-.09	.06	.04	52
1976–1978	.24		-.19	-.04	.45b	.21	53
		-.28a	-.19	-.08	.33a	.23	53
			Internal War				
1967–1969	.02		.08	-.16	-.05	.02	53
		-.19	.12	-.17	.09	.06	53
1970–1972	.10		.02	.22	-.05	.06	53
		-.06	.02	.20	-.09	.06	53
1973–1975	.08		-.05	.23	-.04	.06	52
		-.24	.05	.22	-.09	.10	52
1976–1978	-.03		-.05	-.07	-.08	.01	53
		-.21	-.05	-.07	-.10	.05	53

Note: Beta weights are reported. a p<.05, b p<.01, c p<.001, d p<.0001

regarded more calmly and are seen as contributing to local development efforts and may even be viewed as a form of compensation for past domination. These considerations appear to be most evident when the investments are in the manufacturing sector. These results strongly imply that investments that originate in the United States provoke the sorts of imperialist outcrys that international theorists write about and that these activities are expressed in the form of

Table 4.4
Interaction of Agricultural Investments and the United States and the Colonial Master

Time Period	U.S. x ForInv	Colonial x ForInv	Repress	GovExp	Pop	R2	N
			Protest				
1967–1969	.10		.21	-.38b	.12	.15	63
		-.10	.20	-.37b	.08	.16	63
1970–1972	.54d		.09	-.13	.27a	.32	63
		-.27a	.03	-.19	.09	.14	63
1973–1975	.35b		-.05	-.21	.33b	.25	63
		-.17	-.11	-.24a	.20	.18	63
1976–1978	.33a		-.02	.06	.49c	.24	63
		-.42c	-.17	.07	.38b	.30	63
			Turmoil				
1967–1969	-.10		-.03	-.13	.16	.07	60
		-.09	.03	-.14	.18	.07	60
1970–1972	.15		.08	-.12	.06	.04	60
		-.19	.06	-.07	.01	.05	60
1973–1975	-.11		-.18	-.07	.08	.06	59
		.34a	-.17	-.14	.12	.16	59
1976–1978	.12		-.20	-.06	.48c	.23	60
		.01	-.22	-.06	.45c	.21	60
			Internal War				
1967–1969	-.05		.08	-.15	-.09	.03	60
		-.06	.11	-.15	-.08	.03	60
1970–1972	-.14		-.02	.15	-.18	.06	60
		-.19	-.03	.18	-.13	.08	60
1973–1975	.13		-.05	.19	-.05	.07	59
		-.13	-.08	.22	-.10	.07	59
1976–1978	-.13		-.10	-.08	-.10	.03	60
		-.19	-.14	-.05	-.05	.05	60

Note: Beta weights are reported. a $p<.05$, b $p<.01$, c $p<.001$, d $p<.0001$

protest. At the same time, these findings indicate that those scholars who describe investments from the former colonial master as leading to anti-imperialist reactions are mistaken. There is virtually no evidence to support this assertion.

The next set of findings in Tables 4.5, 4.6, and 4.7 pertain to the date of independence and percentage from the largest foreign national source interaction

Table 4.5
Interaction of Manufacturing Investments and New States and Percentage from the Largest Source

Time Period	New x ForInv	Percent x ForInv	Repress	GovExp	Pop	R2	N
			Protest				
1967–	-.36b		-.06	-.31a	-.07	.23	62
1969		-.27	-.15	-.32a	-.07	.17	57
1970–	-.29a		.01	-.25a	-.01	.15	62
1972		-.18	-.05	-.24	.14	.13	57
1973–	-.23		-.14	-.14	.10	.12	61
1975		-.11	-.15	-.23	.17	.14	57
1976–	-.34b		-.15	.13	.17	.18	62
1978		-.20	-.08	-.05	.13	.07	57
			Turmoil				
1967–	-.23		-.07	-.13	.12	.11	62
1969		-.15	-.10	-.13	.08	.06	57
1970–	-.34a		-.18	.11	-.13	.14	62
1972		-.20	.07	-.14	-.07	.06	57
1973–	-.03		-.12	-.03	.10	.03	61
1975		.02	-.16	-.11	.08	.05	57
1976–	-.12		-.29a	.02	.38b	.21	62
1978		.03	-.21	-.09	.35a	.17	57
			Internal War				
1967–	-.15		.04	-.15	-.12	.05	62
1969		.05	.07	-.17	-.11	.04	57
1970–	-.09		.00	.12	-.15	.04	62
1972		-.05	-.04	.13	-.21	.07	57
1973–	.04		-.11	.17	-.08	.05	61
1975		.09	-.09	.20	-.12	.08	57
1976–	-.07		-.07	-.10	-.08	.02	62
1978		-.01	-.06	-.09	-.12	.02	57

Note: Beta weights are reported. a p<.05, b P,.01, c p<.001, d P<.0001

terms. Once again, the results reveal that protest is most affected, that turmoil is intermittently affected, and that internal war is not affected at all. Manufacturing investments have the most consistent relationship with protest. Table 4.5 shows that the interaction between date of independence and manufacturing investments is negatively related to protest in every time period except 1973–1975. The percentage interaction term for manufacturing is not related

Table 4.6
Interaction of Mining Investments and New States and Percentage from the Largest Source

Time Period	New x ForInv	Percent x ForInv	Repress	GovExp	Pop	R2	N
		Protest					
1967–	-.09		.04	-.39b	-.05	.14	59
1969		.43b	.09	-.30a	.16	.27	56
1970–	-.16		.11	-.27a	.00	.11	59
1972		.09	-.01	-.22	.22	.11	56
1973–	-.11		-.08	-.17	.10	.08	58
1975		.26	-.09	-.18	.29a	.18	56
1976–	-.26		-.09	.12	.16	.12	59
1978		.43b	.00	.05	.34	.21	56
		Turmoil					
1967–	-.17		.02	-.18	.12	.09	59
1969		.02	-.02	-.12	.16	.05	56
1970–	-.28a		-.10	.09	-.14	.11	59
1972		.32a	.13	-.09	.08	.12	56
1973–	-.21		.00	-.03	.06	.05	58
1975		.03	-.15	-.12	.07	.05	56
1976–	-.27a		-.27a	.01	.33a	.25	59
1978		.11	-.19	-.07	.37	.18	56
		Internal War					
1967–	-.18		.07	-.18	-.13	.06	59
1969		-.04	.04	-.17	-.13	.03	56
1970–	-.07		.03	.17	-.13	.05	59
1972		.09	-.03	.15	-.15	.07	56
1973–	-.19		.00	.17	-.13	.07	58
1975		.02	-.09	.21	-.12	.07	56
1976–	-.22		-.02	-.09	-.12	.06	59
1978		-.07	-.07	-.10	-.13	.02	56

Note: Beta weights are reported. a $p<.05$, b $p<.01$, c $p<.001$, d $p<.0001$

to protest. The only other significant result in this table is the negative association between the date of independence term and turmoil during 1970–1972.

The results for the date of independence and percentage interaction terms for mining in Table 4.6 reveal that in newer states, mining investments generally are not related to conflict. The only exceptions are the relatively weak negative relationships found for turmoil in 1970–1972 and 1976–1978, indicating that

Table 4.7
Interaction of Agricultural Investments and New States and Percentage from the Largest Source

Time Period	New x ForInv	Percent x ForInv	Repress	GovExp	Pop	R2	N
			Protest				
1967–	.16		.12	–.40b	.05	.14	62
1969		.27	.06	–.39b	.10	.17	57
1970–	.03		.04	–.26	.07	.07	62
1972		.07	–.01	–.24	.22	.11	57
1973–	.19		–.10	–.18	.20	.10	61
1975		.30a	–.07	–.26a	.30	.20	57
1976–	–.09		–.13	.14	.23	.08	62
1978		.10	–.03	–.03	.22	.05	57
			Turmoil				
1967–	–.16		–.05	–.12	.13	.08	62
1969		–.14	–.09	–.10	.09	.06	57
1970–	–.11		–.15	.12	–.07	.05	62
1972		.15	.17	–.11	–.02	.05	57
1973–	.01		–.12	–.03	.11	.03	61
1975		.21	–.14	–.08	.11	.08	57
1976–	.02		–.27a	.02	.41b	.20	62
1978		.03	–.20	–.09	.36a	.17	57
			Internal War				
1967–	–.08		.07	–.15	–.10	.04	62
1969		–.12	.01	–.14	–.16	.05	57
1970–	–.23		.01	.15	–.19	.08	62
1972		–.19	–.05	.16	–.25	.09	57
1972–	.11		–.08	.15	–.06	.06	61
1975		.08	–.07	–.01	–.11	.03	57
1976–	–.19		–.11	–.08	–.10	.05	62
1978		–.19	–.13	–.08	–.17	.05	57

Note: Beta weights are reported. a p<.05, b p<.01, c p<.001, d p<.0001

during these periods higher levels of mining investments in newer states were mildly associated with less turoil, not more, as the imperialist literature argues.

The percentage interaction term for mining is more strongly related to protest, with relatively strong positive associations in 1967–1969 and in 1976–1978. The only other significant finding for this term is the positive relationship with turmoil in 1970–1972. These results imply that mining investments that are overwhelmingly from a single foreign national source create controversy when times are good or getting better, for 1967–1969 was a period of international prosperity and 1976–1978 was a period of recovery from an earlier recession. At other times, however, when things are more uncertain, these investments do not appear nearly so troublesome. Imperialist arguments about mining investments may be only partially accurate, for the conditions prevailing in the international system seem to play an important role.

The last set of results for the date of independence and percentage interaction terms are for agricultural investments. These are in Table 4.7. With the exception of a modest positive relationship between the percentage interaction term and protest in 1973–1975, the agricultural terms are not related to political conflict. These results suggest that in new states and in states that have a high concentration of investments from one foreign national source, agricultural investments are not responsible for such antiforeign outbursts as may occur.

The final results are for the ethnonationalist interaction terms. These are in Tables 4.8, 4.9, and 4.10. In comparison to some of the imperialist results, these findings are weak. Table 4.8 shows that the manufacturing interaction term is negatively related to protest in 1970–1972 and 1976–1978 and that it is not related to turmoil or internal war. In Table 4.9, one finds that the mining interaction term is not related to protest and internal war and that it has only a modest negative association with turmoil in 1976–1978. Last, the agricultural results in Table 4.10 reveal a negative relationship with protest in 1976–1978 and no associations between this interaction term and turmoil and internal war. In general, these findings imply that foreign investments do not interact with a high degree of ethnonationalist heterogeneity to produce greater levels of conflict. To the extent that there are any effects, they run in the opposite direction, for higher levels of foreign investments in more heterogeneous societies are associated with lower levels of protest and turmoil.

Before turning to the conclusions, it is worth noting the effects of the control variables. The most pronounced of these is the negative relationship between government expenditures and protest in 1967–1969 and the postive relationship between population and both protest and turmoil in 1976–1978. Each of these relationships conforms closely to the effects that these variables were found to have on conflict in earlier chapters.

CHAPTER SUMMARY

This chapter explores the many claims found in the international political economy literature that foreign investments are responsible for producing higher levels of nationalist-based domestic political conflict in developing countries. Three basic models of the connection between foreign investment and nationalist conflict are explored. The first suggested that foreign investments interact with large-scale and fundamental social change to produce political trouble. The second was premised on the contention that foreign investments produce xenophobic conflict by appearing as a part of a foreign

Table 4.8
Interaction of Manufacturing Investments and Ethnonationalism

Time Period	Ethno x ForInv	Repress	GovExp	Pop	R2	N
			Protest			
1967–1969	−.09	.10	−.34a	−.02	.13	61
1970–1972	−.28a	.07	−.20	.04	.15	61
1973–1975	−.08	−.18	−.12	.12	.08	60
1976–1978	−.29a	−.17	.18	.22	.15	61
			Turmoil			
1967–1969	.02	.03	−.17	.15	.05	61
1970–1972	−.21	−.13	.14	−.06	.08	61
1973–1975	.01	−.11	−.03	.11	.03	60
1976–1978	−.06	−.27a	.03	.41b	.20	61
			Internal War			
1967–1969	−.02	.08	−.17	−.07	.03	61
1970–1972	−.10	.02	.13	−.13	.04	61
1973–1975	.11	−.10	.15	−.08	.06	60
1976–1978	.03	−.05	−.11	−.05	.01	61

Note: Beta weights are reported. a p<.05, b p<.01, c p<.001, d p<.0001

inspired scheme that is designed to subjugate developing countries and create a new and subtle form of imperialism. The third was built around the idea that when foreign investors enter societies that are divided along ethnonationalist lines and that are very heterogeneous, they are perceived as favoring some ethnonationalist groups over others and will become the source of controversy and conflict.

Table 4.9
Interaction of Mining Investments and Ethnonationalism

Time Period	Ethno x ForInv	Repress	GovExp	Pop	R2	N
			Protest			
1967–1969	-.11	.11	-.38b	-.06	.14	59
1970–1972	-.24	.09	-.25	.03	.14	59
1973–1975	-.02	-.16	-.14	.10	.06	58
1976–1978	-.25	-.17	.14	.21	.12	59
			Turmoil			
1967–1969	-.01	.07	-.17	.15	.06	59
1970–1972	-.22	-.14	.11	-.08	.08	59
1973–1975	-.13	-.12	-.03	.08	.04	58
1976–1978	-.35b	-.34b	.02	.39b	.29	59
			Internal War			
1967–1969	-.09	.06	-.17	-.08	.03	59
1970–1972	.02	.04	.11	-.14	.04	59
1973–1975	-.12	-.11	.17	-.11	.06	58
1976–1978	-.17	-.07	-.10	-.08	.04	59

Note: Beta weights are reported. a $p<.05$, b $p<.01$, c $p<.001$, d $p<.0001$

Only partial support for any of these expectations was uncovered when these models were tested empirically. The change-oriented model received almost no support. This was true across each of the four time periods and for all three of the types of domestic conflict that were investigated. There simply is little evidence to support the idea that when foreign investments are introduced into a society that is in a state of rapid change, the end product is

Table 4.10
Interaction of Agricultural Investments and Ethnonationalism

Time Period	Ethno x ForInv	Repress	GovExp	Pop	R2	N
			Protest			
1967–1969	−.03	.19	−.40b	.07	.15	65
1970–1972	−.23	.01	−.21	.07	.12	65
1973–1975	−.10	−.09	−.20	.19	.12	65
1976–1978	−.36b	−.23	.18	.25a	.20	65
			Turmoil			
1967–1969	−.11	−.02	−.14	.15	.07	62
1970–1972	−.09	−.16	.12	−.07	.05	62
1973–1975	.04	−.11	−.04	.12	.03	61
1976–1978	−.03	−.28a	.03	.40b	.20	62
			Internal War			
1967–1969	−.04	.08	−.16	−.09	.03	62
1970–1972	−.20	.00	.16	−.17	.07	62
1973–1975	.15	−.07	.14	−.05	.07	61
1976–1978	−.16	−.10	−.08	−.09	.04	62

Note: Beta weights are reported. a $p<.05$, b $p<.01$, c $p<.001$, d $p<.0001$

a greater level of political conflict. These findings conform with and extend the findings of other researchers who have found no reason to believe that rapid social change in itself is a key to conflict. The results from this analysis indicate that basic social changes do not lead to greater levels of conflict even when there is the sort of large foreign presence that some social theorists argue should produce outbursts of xenophobic political activity.

The examination of the imperialist arguments about how foreign investments might lead to nationalist conflict produced interesting results, some of them unexpected in light of the arguments found in the literature. The first surprise was that manufacturing investments, as opposed to investments in mining and agriculture, appeared to be the most potent type of investment for creating conflict. This does not mean that mining and agricultural investments had no effects on conflict, but it does mean that manufacturing investments produced generally stronger and more consistent results across each of the time periods examined. These results run directly contrary to the expectations derived from the international political economy literature that point to investments in primary products as most likely to heighten the sense of exploitation that is supposedly at the core of the nationalist conflict resulting from the belief that one is under the thumb of imperialists.

A second surprise is found in the results for new states and for those where foreign investments are primarily from the former colonial overlord. Imperialist arguments expected that for these states, higher levels of investments would be associated with greater levels of conflict. In fact, the results indicated that higher levels of investments were associated with lower levels of conflict (primarily protest), with the most consistent results appearing when manufacturing investments were examined. One reason for this was that manufacturing investments might be perceived in the host state as a partial payment for past exploitation, and these investments might be seen as likely to assist in promoting economic growth and development. Another explanation also is possible. This is that multinational manufacturing firms tend to invest in areas that they regard as stable, and that ex-colonies that display a reasonable degree of political and social stability are natural investment outlets for those who wish to do business in the developing world. In other words, causation may run from stability to investments instead of from investments to stability. Both of these possibilities deserve attention in future research.

Another interesting finding from the analysis of the imperialist model was that among countries that receive most of their investments from the United States, there is a consistent tendency for higher investments to be related to greater levels of political protest, particularly when the investments are in manufacturing. This finding conforms to the expectations of some imperialist theorists who maintain that U.S. investments are a special source of concern in the developing world because the strength of the United States creates the fear of possible domination whenever a society is too closely tied either to the American government or to visible and potentially powerful agents of American culture. Future research should explore the degree to which these patterns have persisted in the more immediate past and, in particular, the post–Cold War period.

The last result relating to imperialism has to do with the degree to which one's investments are overwhelmingly from a single foreign national source, indicating that one is enmeshed in a feudal pattern of international interactions (Galtung 1971). The results for this variable were inconsistent. Only mining investments revealed any reasonably strong relationships, with greater levels of mining investments associated with higher levels of protest during periods of prosperity and recovery. This implies two things. First, highly concentrated mining investments only are a source of trouble in good times. When things go bad, there is little tendency to attack foreign corporations. Second, in light of the results for the United States and the former colonial master variables, one might reasonably conclude that the key variable is not whether you have a high concentration of investments from one source, but is who that source is.

A final comment is in order about the ethnonationalist results. These results were both weak and inconsistent. It is true that there were some significant relationships here and there between each of the foreign investment variables and protest and turmoil. However, no clear patterns of relationships emerged. In fact, to the extent that the ethnonationalist variables were related to conflict, the findings revealed that among more diverse countries, higher levels of foreign investments were related to less conflict. This runs directly contrary to the arguments in the literature.[12]

The results from this chapter clearly were strongest when the imperialist arguments were examined. For the most part, they revealed that manufacturing investments were most firmly related to conflict and that among the forms of conflict studied, protest was the most affected. In general, the imperialist expectations were most accurate as far as their claims about the United States as an investment source were concerned. Imperialist claims were inaccurate in their descriptions of how new states and those with their investments from the former colonial master would be affected by foreign investments, for investments in these states appear as a possible source of stability, as opposed to the instability that imperialists expect. Finally, there is little evidence to support the arguments of those who state that conflict results from the high concentrations of investments that are a product of feudal interaction patterns.

NOTES

1. Extensive discussions of how multinational corporations are the target of anti-foreign hostility are found in Barnet and Muller 1974, Moran 1978, Pinelo 1973, Sklar 1975, and Vernon 1971.

2. The collapse of the European empires after World War II produced a vast literature that examined the domestic and foreign policy behavior patterns of the new states. For further discussions of the many issues associated with the subject, see Brecher 1963; Good 1962; LaFever 1962; Liska 1962, 1968; Mates 1972; and Rothstein 1968, 1977.

3. One of the central issues in the international relations literature has for years centered around the definition of the nation, the ethnic group, and related concepts. Connor (1993), Banton (1983), and Rothschild (1981) provide excellent discussions of the definitional problems surrounding these concepts. For the purposes of this presentation, an ethnonationalist group will be defined as a segment of a state's population that regards itself as culturally distinct from other parts of the state's population, that sees itself as having its own traditions and heritage, that often shares a common language

and religion, and that has a political agenda of its own, which may include independence or may be of a more limited nature.

4. The nationalist arguments in this chapter assert that foreign investments in the manufacturing, mining, and agricultural sectors all interact with certain nationalist characteristics of the host society to affect conflict. Investments in each of these sectors are examined. Foreign investments are measured. The stock of foreign investment in the sector examined is weighted by the total GDP of the host state that is derived from that sector. Investment data by sector are from the same source used earlier, as are the data pertaining to GDP. These variables were measured only for 1967 because data for other years were not available.

5. The values for these variables only are available for 1965, 1970, 1975, and 1980. The figures for 1965–1970 were used for the 1967–1969 period, those for 1970–1975 were used for the 1970–1972 and 1973–1975 periods, and those for 1975–1980 were used for the 1976–1978 period.

6. The Atlas Narodov Mira score for this variable was used in preference to the other scores provided by Taylor and Hudson (1972) because it is available for a greater number of the countries in the present data set. This score for assessing ethnonational heterogenity was for circa 1965. The basic stability of this variable should insure that the use of data for this year will not distort the results one obtains when analyzing later points in time. For a complete discussion of this score and how it is constructed, see Taylor and Hudson 1972.

7. The use of this variable to measure ethnonationalism is built on the assumption that the larger the sheer number of ethnonationalist groups contained in a society, the greater the probability of conflict. It is possible to argue that it is not the sheer number of such groups but the depth of the antagonism between these groups that accounts for conflict. Unfortunately, systematic data that measure the degree of animosity between ethnonational groups are not available. In order to determine whether larger numbers of ethnonationalist groups are a key to conflict, regression analysis was performed to assess how the ethnolinguistic fractionalization measure was related to protest, turmoil, and internal war. The results revealed strong effects on protest that conformed to the assumption that larger numbers of groups produce more conflict. There were few effects on turmoil and internal war. These findings conform closely to those reported by Hibbs (1973, 76–78). The basic assumption behind the use of this measure for ethnonational divisions appears reasonable. Still, these results should be regarded as preliminary. Additional research that employs more complex measures of the antagonism between groups should be pursued in the future.

8. An additional interaction term was created that was based on achieving independence after 1960, the year when the single largest contingent of ex-colonies gained their independence. This allowed for a check to determine whether using 1945 to distinguish new states from old created unusual results. In both cases, the results were substantially the same.

9. As is the case in Chapter 3, additional dummy variables are created based on the use of the upper quartile to define high values. These variables are used to determine whether the results obtained for dummy variables based on the median were unusual. In all cases, the results for the upper quartile variables were essentially the same as those that are reported.

10. It is realized that the main effects of mining investments were not considered earlier. These results are not reported in this chapter because the primary theoretical

concern is with the interaction effects. These results are available from the author upon request.

11. In addition to manufacturing investments, those in mining and agriculture also were examined as a check to insure that the patterns of relationships for these sectors were consistent with the patterns found for the manufacturing sector. In all cases, the patterns were essentially the same.

12. See Hibbs (1973, 76–78), who found that greater ethnonational divisions interact with social change to produce more political protest.

CHAPTER 5

SUMMARY AND CONCLUSIONS

This book investigates how the international interdependence stemming from direct foreign investments affects the political conflict and violence found in developing countries. This topic was examined because of the importance that such conflicts have for international peace and commercial stability and because of the negative implications that social disruptions have for growth and development in poor countries. Many recent international approaches to the promotion of economic progress in the developing world stress growing levels of interdependence as a means for overcoming the deficiencies that are found in many of the world's most disadvantaged countries. If interdependence is responsible for conflict, then it is possible that these ideas about how to best promote progress are very misguided.

Three basic models of the relationship between foreign investments and domestic conflict are examined. The first was built around the notion that interdependence produces conflict by way of a deprivation process, wherein conflict is the result of the deep-seated resentment that some members of society feel when they believe that they have been denied what they regard as their fair share of the society's resources. The results pertaining to this model were mixed. On the one hand, there was support for the argument that stocks of foreign manufacturing investments contribute to both relative and absolute deprivation mechanisms, with the former appearing among Latin American countries in the years of prosperity found in the late 1960s and the latter emerging among sub-Saharan African countries during the economically troubled period of the late 1970s. On the other hand, higher flows of foreign investments were associated with lower levels of violent conflict in Asia in the late 1970s and stocks of foreign manufacturing investments consistently were related to lesser amounts of political protest in Africa across all of the time periods explored. Stocks of foreign agricultural investments seemed to ameliorate the tendency toward agrarian conflict in Africa.

On the basis of these findings, one might conclude that foreign investments both exacerbate and retard deprivation processes. Foreign investments create a greater probability of relative deprivation conflict among the relatively wealthy and more established societies of Latin America during periods of international expansion. They also increase the chance that absolute deprivation will produce conflict, but only among the very poor and newly independent countries of Africa during times of international economic downturns. In each case, the result is higher levels of internal war. At the same time, one finds that foreign investments in both manufacturing and in agriculture reduce the likelihood of nonviolent political protest in African states. In other words, foreign investments constitute a mixed blessing as far as deprivation processes are concerned.

The second model explored in this book focuses on the degree to which foreign investments interact with social change to produce political conflict. This is the mobilization model. The basic premise behind this model was the hypothesis that social changes produce winners and losers, and that both groups will react to their altered circumstances by seeking to push political authorities toward policies that will help them to cope with their new environment. The empirical findings in Chapter 3 strongly supports these arguments. It was found that mobilization conflict occurs most readily in those developing societies where information flows with relative ease and where people are best able to form groups to pursue common interests. The results also implied that specific groups, most notably workers in industry and petite entrepreneurs, are likely to view conflict as an appropriate method for securing policy adjustments from the government, with the working class appearing to push for proactive policies that are designed to bring new privileges, while entrepreneurs apparently seek reactive policies to protect them from international competition. In these circumstances, the results indicate that the effects of conflict are consistent across each of the time periods examined. Another interesting finding suggests that the most powerful domestic business interests in developing countries also are prone toward promoting conflict when international markets stagnate and competition becomes more intense. In each case, the type of conflict that is most affected is political protest, for the affected actors appear most concerned with altering policy instead of destroying one government and replacing it with another.

The final model examined in this book has to do with whether foreign investments produced greater levels of conflict by interacting with certain types of nationalist characteristics that are often found in developing societies. In this case, there was virtually no support for arguments that linked foreign investments to conflict by way of an interaction with either the fundamental social changes or ethnonationalist divisions in a country. The imperialist results show that foreign manufacturing investments are associated with less conflict in new states and in societies where the former imperial overlord continues to play a leading role. Each of these findings runs directly counter to the expectations of those who hypothesize that foreign investments interact with nationalist forces in the host society to produce conflict. The only result that conformed to nationalist expectations was the finding that higher levels of foreign investments (primarily in manufacturing and agriculture) were related to greater levels of conflict in cases where the investments were primarily from the United States. Once again, political protest was the form of conflict that was most affected.

The results from the investigation of these models contain both good news and bad news for those concerned with the issue of how interdependence affects domestic conflict. One part of the good news is found in the fact that foreign investments do not appear to provoke much of the sort of high-level violent conflict (internal war) that has tended in the past to lead to foreign intervention and international commercial instability and that is most frequently described as undermining attempts at development. Foreign investments only are associated with greater levels of this type of conflict under very limited international conditions and among certain groups of states, which means that these effects are closely bounded both in time and in space. Relative deprivation effects leading to internal war were limited to Latin America during one three-year period of time, while absolute deprivation was associated with more violence only in Africa during the late 1970s. There were, however, no general and persistent patterns of effects that connected foreign investments with internal war.

Another piece of good news is a product of the relationship whereby foreign investments consistently are related to lower levels of political protest in new states (many of which are in Africa) and in countries where the former imperial overlord plays a leading role. Foreign agricultural investments in the poverty-stricken states of sub-Saharan Africa appear to bring stability to the agrarian sector and to reduce the incidence of protest. In each case, foreign investments may be regarded as contributing to at least one aspect of the political conditions that are required for the promotion of economic growth and development. The effects of agricultural investments are particularly significant in light of the role that the agrarian sector plays in many developing countries, especially in Africa. It is also worth noting that these effects among African states are consistent across each of the time periods examined.

As for the bad news, this is found in the tendency for higher levels of foreign investment, especially in the manufacturing sector, to be related to higher levels of political protest in societies with better-developed communications structures, where people can interact more easily, and when the investments are predominantly from the United States. Industrial workers and entrepreneurs, both large and small, are prone toward encouraging and participating in protest when a society has higher stocks of maufacturing investments.

Foreign investments apparently do provoke a greater degree of the sort of conflict that can create an unsettling political environment and that may lead to an on-again, off-again approach to the formation and implementation of policies that are designed to promote economic growth and development. Foreign investments seem to contribute to a situation in which protest may force the government to choose between consistent policy and efforts to appease the often contradictory demands for proactive and reactive government actions that are made by the various groups that are affected by the foreign presence. In considering this point, one should remember that calls for proactive and reactive policy place very different demands on government authorities. Those favoring reactive behavior tend to demand protection that limits the role of foreigners, while those pushing for proactive policy usually accept the foreign presence and want to see it enlarged, wishing only for greater privileges for themselves as their importance to society increases in conjunction with growing levels of interdependence. The government is faced with increasingly complex and tough political choices. Interdependence seems to muddy the political climate to a substantial degree by helping to create and unleash political forces that pull and tug the government in different directions and that confront the government with the prospect of continual demonstrations, albeit peaceful, no matter what course of action it selects.

One can draw two basic conclusions from this research. The first is that foreign investments generally serve as a source of political stability in the poorest and most recently independent parts of the developing world, especially during periods of international prosperity. The second is that somewhat more advanced developing societies that have better communications facilities and larger numbers of well-organized and politically oriented factions and groups are likely to confront a substantial and ongoing increase in their levels of political protest when they are the host of higher quantities of foreign investment.

Having said this, it should be recognized that the absolute levels of foreign investment in the newer and poorest states tends to be small in comparison to the amounts found in the more advanced parts of the Third World. One might also conclude that the nature of the impact of foreign investment on political protest also depends upon how pervasive these investments are in the host society. When the absolute levels are relatively low, the total numbers of those affected by the foreign presence also should be low, and an increase in the amount of investment may act as a source of stability by creating the general perception among key political actors that the social situation is improving.

Where the absolute level is much higher, the total number of the affected will be much greater, and larger quantities of investments may simply contribute to a greater overall feeling of concern that foreigners are playing too great a role in society (particularly when the investments are from the United States) and have become too much of a threat to the social, political, and economic positions of politically vocal elements within the host state. At the same time, larger absolute levels increase the degree to which many members of the host society benefit from the foreigners and will be inclined toward proactive behavior.

These conclusions suggest that development strategies that are based on the promotion of international interdependence are least likely to upset the political stability of the poorest and newest countries in the Third World. Unfortunately, these are the very countries where multinational corporations are most hesitant to put their money because the prospects for an acceptable profit are dimmest. At the same time, the political climate in wealthier countries, which are the societies where international firms generally are most prepared to invest, is much more likely to be adversely affected by a strategy that calls for increased levels of international interdependence. As is so often the case in the real world of international politics, those societies that might benefit the most and suffer the least from policies built around increasing interdependence might be unable to make the proper use of the policy because of their inability to attract foreign firms because of their general poverty, while those states that will benefit the least and suffer the most from the policy in question can pursue it much more freely because foreigners are more willing to invest in their better-developed and more profitable environments.

This research serves as a first step down the long road to exploring the many domestic political consequences that are associated with the rapidly expanding international interdependence that has appeared and accelerated in the years since World War II. Future research should focus on at least three questions. The first relates to the exploration of additional time periods, especially the years since the end of the Cold War. It would be particularly instructive to see whether new patterns of interdependence are emerging in the wake of that contest and how the end of the East–West conflict has affected the perceptions that many have of international imperialism.

A second area for research should examine in greater depth the reactions of the many differing types of organizations and groups that are found within any society to increasing levels of foreign penetration. The research reported herein has only begun to tap this question. Much more detailed work should be pursued in order to develop a better theoretical portrait of the effects of interdependence and to provide policy makers with more accurate guideposts for decision making. This takes on special importance in light of the growing tendency toward closer economic ties among many of the world's nations. Policy makers need to know more about the political behavior they can expect to confront as they proceed along the path to higher levels of interdependence.

Finally, it is important that further research consider the political effects of additional forms of interdependence. This book considers one of the most important types, direct foreign investments. Many others also should be explored. In particular, trade, external loans, and portfolio investments should be examined carefully. Each of these forms of interdependence has grown and is growing very rapidly. And each can be expected to have effects that at the same time are far-reaching and are different from the effects of direct foreign investments. Once again, it is vital that governments, policy analysts, and scholars understand exactly what the impacts of varying forms of interdependence are if they are to chart an appropriate course in the years of change that are ahead.

STATES IN THE DATA SET

Afghanistan	El Salvador	Madagascar	Singapore
Algeria	Ethiopia	Malawi	Somalia
Angola	Ghana	Malaysia	Spain
Argentina	Greece	Mali	Sri Lanka
Bangladesh	Guatemala	Mauritania	Sudan
Benin	Guinea	Mexico	Syria
Bolivia	Haiti	Mongolia	Tanzania
Brazil	Honduras	Morocco	Thailand
Burkina Faso	Hong Kong	Mozambique	Togo
Burma	India	Nicaragua	Trinidad
Burundi	Indonesia	Niger	Tunisia
Cambodia	Iran	Nigeria	Turkey
Cameroon	Iraq	Pakistan	Uganda
Central African Republic	Ireland	Papua New Guinea	Uruguay
Chad	Ivory Coast	Paraguay	Venezuela
Chile	Jamaica	Peru	North Yemen
Colombia	Jordan	Philippines	South Yemen
Costa Rica	Kenya	Portugal	Yugoslavia
Dominican Republic	South Korea	Rwanda	Zaire
Ecuador	Laos	Senegal	Zambia
Egypt	Lebanon	Sierra Leone	Zimbabwe

DATA SOURCES

Variable	Indicator	Source
Stock of foreign investment in manufacturing, mining, and agriculture	Measured in U.S. dollars for 1967	1
Flows of foreign investment	Measured in U.S. dollars for 1967–1971	1
Percentage of foreign investment from the United States, the largest foreign source, and the former colonial master	Measured for 1967	1
Internal war, turmoil, protest, reform, and repression	Measured for 1967–1969, 1970–1972,1973–1975, and 1976–1978	2
Government expenditures	Measured in U.S. dollars for 1967	3
Percentage of the population in the agricultural labor force	Measured for 1965, 1970, 1975, and 1980	4
Percentage of of the labor force in industry	Measured for 1965, 1970, 1975, and 1980	4
Percentage of the population living in urban areas	Measured for 1965, 1970, 1975, and 1980	4
Percentage of the secondary school age population in school	Measured for 1970	4
Radios per 1,000 population	Measured for 1970	4

Variable	Indicator	Source
Total population	Measured for 1967	5
Total GDP and GDP in mining, manufacturing, and agriculture	Measured in U.S. dollars for 1967	6
Real growth in GDP per capita and in industry	Measured for 1967–1969, 1970–1972, 1973–1975, and 1976–1978	6
Income inequality	Measured for 1965–1970	4
Democracy versus nondemocracy	Measured for 1967–1969, 1970–1972, 1973–1975, and1976–1978	7
Percentage of GDP in manufacturing	Measured for 1967, 1970, 1973, and 1976	6
Manufacturing as a percentage of total exports	Measured for 1967, 1970, 1973, and 1976	4
Change in terms of trade	Measured for 1967–1969, 1970–1972, 1973–1975, and 1976–1978	4
Trade as a percentage of GDP	Measured for 1967, 1970, 1973, and 1976	6
Ethnolinguistic fractionalization	Measured for 1965	8
Freedom of the press	Measured for 1973–1979	9
Organized labor as a percentage of total labor	Measured for 1975	9
Date of independence	Year of independence	10

1 = OECD, *Stock of Private Direct Investment by DAC Countries in Developing Countries*, Update. Paris: OECD, microfiche, no date.

2 = Conflict and Peace Data Bank Domestic Scale

3 = U.S. Arms Control and Disarmament Agency, *World Military Expenditures and Arms Transfers*, various years.

4 = World Bank, *World Tables*, various years.

5 = United Nations, *Demographic Yearbook*, various years.

6 = United Nations, *Yearbook of National Accounts Statistics*, various years.

7 = Author coded as described in Chapter 3, footnote 8.

8 = Charles Taylor and Michael Hudson, *World Handbook of Political and Social Indicators II*. New Haven, Conn.: Yale University Press, 1972.

9 = Charles Taylor and David Jodice, *World Handbook of Political and Social Indicators III*. New Haven, Conn.: Yale University Press, 1983.

10 = Arthur Banks, *Political Handbook of the World*. New York: McGraw-Hill, various years.

REFERENCES

Allison, Paul D. 1977. "Testing for Interaction in Multiple Regression." *American Journal of Sociology* 83 (July): 144–153.

Alschuler, Lawrence R. 1988. *Multinationals and Maldevelopment.* New York: St. Martin's Press.

Althauser, Robert P. 1971. "Multicollinearity and Non-Additive Regression Models." Pp. 453–472 in *Causal Models in the Social Sciences*, H. M. Blalock, Jr., ed. Chicago: Aldine-Atherton.

Ananaba, Wogu. 1979. *The Trade Union Movement in Africa.* London: C. Hurst and Co.

Anderson, Leslie E. 1990. "Post-Materialism from a Peasant Perspective: Political Motivation in Costa Rica and Nicaragua." *Comparative Political Studies* 23 (April): 80–113.

Aristotle. 1971. "Politics." Pp. 86–88 in *When Men Revolt and Why*, James C. Davies, ed. New York: Free Press.

Armstrong, Adrienne. 1981. "Political Consequences of Economic Dependence." *Journal of Conflict Resolution* 25 (September): 401–428.

Asher, Herbert. 1976. *Causal Modeling.* Beverly Hills, Calif.: Sage.

Aya, Rod. 1984. "Popular Intervention in Revolutionary Situations." Pp. 318–343 in *Statemaking and Social Movements: Essays in History and Theory*, Charles Bright and Susan Harding, eds. Ann Arbor: University of Michigan Press.

Ayers, Robert. 1975. "Political Regimes, Explanatory Variables, and Public Policy in Latin America." *The Journal of Developing Areas* 10 (October): 15–35.

Azar, Edward E. 1980. "The Conflict and Peace Data Bank (COPDAB) Project." *Journal of Conflict Resolution* 24 (March): 143–152.

Azar, Edward E. 1982. *The Codebook of the Conflict and Peace Data Bank.* College Park, Md.: Center for International Development.

Banks, Arthur S. 1978. *Political Handbook of the World.* New York: McGraw-Hill.

Banton, Michael. 1983. *Racial and Ethnic Competition.* Cambridge: Cambridge University Press.

Banton, Michael. 1994. "Modeling Ethnic and National Relations." *Ethnic and Racial Studies* 17 (January): 1–19.

Baran, Paul A. 1957. *The Political Economy of Growth.* New York: Monthly Review Press.

Barnet, Richard, and Ronald Muller. 1974. *Global Reach.* New York: Simon and Schuster.

Becker, David G., and Richard L. Sklar. 1987. "Why Post Imperialism?" Pp. 1–18 in *Postimperialism: International Capitalism in the Late Twentieth Century*, David G. Becker, Jeff Frieden, Sayre P. Schatz, and Richard Sklar, eds. Boulder, Colo.: Lynne Rienner Publishers.

Berg-Schlosser, Dirk. 1982. "Modes and Meaning of Political Participation in Kenya." *Comparative Politics* 14 (July): 397–415.

Berry, William, and Stanley Feldman. 1985. *Multiple Regression in Practice.* Beverly Hills, Calif.: Sage Publishers.

Billet, Bret. 1991. *Investment Behavior of Multinational Corporations in Developing Areas.* New Brunswick, N.J.: Transaction Publishers.

Bodenheimer, Susanne. 1971. "Dependency and Inperialism: The Roots of Latin American Underdevelopment." Pp. 155–182 in *Readings in U.S. Imperialism*, K. T. Fann and D. C. Hodges, eds. Boston: Porter Sargent.

Bollen, Kenneth. 1983. "World System Position, Dependency, and Democracy." *American Sociological Review* 48 (August): 468–479.

Bornschier, Volker. 1981. "Dependent Industrialization in the World Economy." *Journal of Conflict Resolution* 25 (September): 371–400.

Bornschier, Volker, and T. Ballmer-Cao. 1979. "Income Inequality: A Cross-National Study of the Relationship between MNC Penetration, Dimensions of the Power Structure, and Income Distribution." *American Sociological Review* 44 (June): 487–506.

Bornschier, Volker, and Christopher Chase-Dunn. 1985. *Transnational Corporations and Development.* New York: Praeger.

Bornschier, Volker, Richard Rubinson, and Christopher Chase-Dunn. 1978. "Cross-National Evidence of the Effects of Foreign Investment and Aid on Economic Growth and Inequality: A Survey of Findings and a Reanalysis." *American Journal of Sociology* 84 (November): 651–683.

Boswell, Terry, and William J. Dixon. 1990. "Dependency and Rebellion: A Cross-National Analysis." *American Sociological Review* 55 (August): 540–559.

Boswell, Terry, and William J. Dixon. 1993. "Marx's Theory of Rebellion: A Cross-National Analysis of Class Exploitation, Economic Development, and Violent Revolt." *American Sociological Review* 58 (October): 681–702.

Brecher, Michael. 1963. *The New States of Asia.* London: Oxford University Press.

Brinton, Crane. 1965. *The Anatomy of Revolution.* New York: Vintage Books.

Brockett, Charles. 1988. *Land, Power, and Poverty.* Boston: Unwin Hyman.

Brockett, Charles. 1991. "The Structure of Political Opportunities and Peasant Mobilization in Central America." *Comparative Politics* 23 (April): 253–274.

Brockett, Charles. 1992. "Measuring Political Violence and Land Inequality in Central America." *American Political Science Review* 86 (March): 169–176.

Brundenius, C. 1972. "The Anatomy of Imperialism: The Case of Multinational Mining Corporations in Peru." *Journal of Peace Research* 9 (3): 189–207.

Burg, Steven L., and Michael L. Berbaum. 1989. "Community, Integration and Stability in Multinational Yugoslavia." *American Political Science Review* 83 (June): 535–554.

Calvocoressi, Peter. 1962. *World Order and New States.* New York: Praeger.

Caporaso, James A. 1978. "Dependence, Dependency, and Power in the Global System: A Structural and Behavioral Analysis." *International Organization* 32 (Winter): 13–43.

Cardoso, Fernando Henrique. 1979. "On the Characterization of Authoritarian Regimes in Latin America." Pp. 33–57 in *The New Authoritarianism in Latin America*, David Collier, ed. Princeton: Princeton University Press.

Cardoso, Fernando Henrique, and Enzo Faletto. 1979. *Dependency and Development in Latin America.* Berkeley: University of California Press.

Chazan, Naomi. 1982. "The New Politics of Participation in Tropical Africa." *Comparative Politics* 14 (January): 169–189.

Chenery, Hollis, and Moises Syrquin. 1975. *Patterns of Development.* New York: Oxford University Press.

Clark, Cal. 1989. "External Shocks and Instability in Taiwan: The Dog that Didn"t Bark." Pp. 173–187 in *Markets, Politics, and Change in the Global Political Economy*, William P. Avery and David P. Rapkin, eds. Boulder, Colo.: Lynne Rienner Publishers.

Collier, David. 1979. "Overview of the Bureaucratic-Authoritarian Model." Pp. 19–32 in *The New Authoritarianism in Latin America*, David Collier, ed. Princeton: Princeton University Press.

Connor, Walker. 1993. "Beyond Reason: The Nature of the Ethnonational Bond." *Ethnic and Racial Studies* 16 (July): 373–389.

Cornelius, Wayne A. 1969. "Urbanization as an Agent in Latin American Political Instability: The Case of Mexico." *American Political Science Review* 63 (September): 833–857.

Crighton, Elizabeth, and Martha Abele MacIver. 1991. "The Evolution of Protracted Ethnic Conflict: Group Dominance and Political Underdevelopment in Northern Ireland and Lebanon." *Comparative Politics* 23 (January): 127–142.

Deutsch, Karl. 1979. *Tides Among Nations.* New York: Free Press.

Deyo, Frederic C. 1981. *Dependent Development and Industrial Order.* New York: Praeger.

Deyo, Frederic C. 1987. "State and Labor: Modes of Political Exclusion in East Asian Development." Pp. 182–202 in *The Political Economy of the New Asian Industrialism*, F. C. Deyo, ed. Ithaca, N.Y.: Cornell University Press.

Diaz-Alejandro, Carlos F. 1970. "Direct Foreign Investment in Latin America." Pp. 319–344 in *The International Corporation*, C. P. Kindleberger, ed. Cambridge, Mass.: MIT Press.

Dix, Robert W. 1983. "The Varieties of Revolution." *Comparative Politics* 15 (April): 281–294.

Dolan, Michael, and Brian Tomlin. 1980. "First World–Third World Linkages: External Relations and Economic Development." *International Organization* 34 (Winter): 41–64.

Dolan, Michael, and Brian Tomlin. 1984. "Foreign Policy in Asymmetrical Dyads: Theoretical Reformulation and Empirical Analysis, Canada–United States Relations, 1963–1972." *International Studies Quarterly* 28 (September): 349–368.

Dolan, Michael, Brian Tomlin, Harold Von Riekhoff, and Maureen A. Molot. 1982. "Asymmetrical Dyads and Foreign Policy: Canada–U.S. Relations, 1963–1972." *Journal of Conflict Resolution* 26 (September): 387–422.

Dos Santos, Theotonio. 1971. "The Structure of Dependence." Pp. 225–236 in *Readings in U.S. Imperialism*, K. T. Fann and D. C. Hodges, eds. Boston: Porter Sargent.

Duvall, Raymond, and John Freeman. 1981. "The State and Dependent Capitalism." *International Studies Quarterly* 25 (March): 99–118.

Duvall, Raymond, and John Freeman. 1983. "The Techno-Bureaucratic Elite and the Entrepreneurial State in Dependent Industrialization." *American Political Science Review* 77 (September): 569–587.

Esman, Milton J. 1987. "Ethnic Politics and Economic Power." *Comparative Politics* 19 (July): 395–418.

Evans, Peter. 1979. *Dependent Development*. Princeton: Princeton University Press.

Evans, Peter. 1987. "Class, State, and Dependence in East Asia: Lessons for Latin Americanists." Pp. 203–226 in *The Political Economy of the New Asian Industrialism*, F. C. Deyo, ed. Ithaca, N.Y.: Cornell University Press.

Fagen, Richard R. 1978. "A Funny Thing Happened on the Way to the Market: Thoughts on Extending Dependency Ideas." *International Organization* 32 (Winter): 287–300.

Feierabend, Ivo K., and Rosalind L. Feierabend. 1966. "Aggressive Behaviors Within Polities, 1948–1962: A Cross-National Study." *Journal of Conflict Resolution* 10 (September): 249–271.

Fireman, Bruce, and William A. Gamson. 1979. "Utilitarian Logic in the Resource Mobilization Perspective." Pp. 8–44 in *The Dynamics of Social Movements*, Mayer N. Zald and John D. McCarthy, eds. Cambridge, Mass.: Winthrop Publishers.

Frank, Isaiah. 1980. *Foreign Enterprise in Developing Countries*. Baltimore: Johns Hopkins University Press.

Freeman, Jo. 1979. "Resource Mobilization and Strategy: A Model for Analyzing Social Movement Organization Actions." Pp. 167–189 in *The Dynamics of Social Movements*, Mayer N. Zald and John D. McCarthy, eds. Cambridge, Mass.: Winthrop Publishers.

Frieden, Jeffrey A. 1981. "Third World Indebted Industrialization: International Finance and State Capitalism in Mexico, Brazil, Algeria, and South Korea." *International Organization* 35 (Summer): 407–432.

Frieden, Jeffrey A. 1987. "International Capital and National Development: Comments on Post-Imperialism." Pp. 179–191 in *Postimperialism: International Capitalism and Development in the Late Twentieth Century*, David G. Becker, Jeff Frieden, Sayre P. Schatz, and Richard Sklar, eds. Boulder, Colo.: Lynne Rienner Publishers.

Frieden, Jeffrey A. 1991. "Invested Interests: The Politics of National Economic Policies in a World of Global Finance." *International Organization* 45 (Autumn): 425–451.

Friedrich, Robert J. 1982. "In Defense of Multiplicative Terms in Multiple Regression Equations." *American Journal of Political Science* 26 (November): 797–833.

Galeano, E. 1971. "Latin America and the Theory of Imperialism." Pp. 205–224 in *Readings in U.S. Imperialism*, K. T. Fann and D. C. Hodges, eds. Boston: Porter Sargent.

Galtung, Johan. 1971. "A Structural Theory of Imperialism." *Journal of Peace Research* 8 (2): 81–117.

Gamson, William A. 1975. *The Strategy of Social Protest*. Homewood, Ill.: Dorsey Press.

Gasiorowski, Mark. 1985. "The Structure of Third World Economic Interdependence." *International Organization* 39 (Spring): 331–342.

Gasiorowski, Mark. 1988. "Economic Dependence and Political Democracy: A Cross-National Study." *Comparative Political Studies* 20 (January): 489–515.

Gastil, Raymond D. 1973. "The New Criteria of Freedom." *Freedom at Issue* 17 (January-February): 2–23.

Gereffi, Gary. 1978. "Drug Firms and Dependency in Mexico: The Case of the Steroid Hormone Industry." *International Organization* 32 (Winter): 237–286.

Gerschwender, James A. 1968. "Explorations in the Theory of Social Movements and Revolutions." *Social Forces* 47 (September): 127–135.

Gilpin, Robert. 1975. *U.S. Power and the Multinational Corporation*. New York: Basic Books.

Gladwin, Thomas, and Ingo Walter. 1980. *Multinationals Under Fire: Lessons in the Management of Conflict*. New York: John Wiley and Sons.

Gold, Thomas B. 1988. "Entrepreneurs, Multinationals, and the State." Pp. 175–205 in *Contending Approaches to the Political Economy of Taiwan*, E. A. Winckler and S. Greenhalgh, eds. London: M. E. Sharpe Publishers.

Goldstone, Jack A. 1980. "Theories of Revolution: The Third Generation." *World Politics* 32 (April): 425–453.

Good, Robert. 1962. "State Building as a Determinant of Foreign Policy in the New States." Pp. 3–12 in *Neutralism and Nonalignment*, L. W. Martin, ed. New York: Praeger.

Gourevitch, Peter. 1978. "The Second Image Reversed: The International Sources of Domestic Politics." *International Organization* 32 (Autumn): 881–912.

Greenhalgh, Susan. 1988. "Supranational Processes of Income Distribution." Pp. 67–100 in *Contending Approaches to the Political Economy of Taiwan*, E. A. Winckler and S. Greenhalgh, eds. London: M. E. Sharpe.

Griffin, Richard W. 1992. "Political Opportunity, Resource Mobilization, and Social Movements: The Case of South Texas Farm Workers." *Social Science Journal* 29 (2): 129–152.

Gurr, Ted Robert. 1968. "A Causal Model of Civil Strife: A Comparative Analysis Using New Indices." *American Political Science Review* 62 (December): 1104–1124.

Gurr, Ted Robert. 1970. *Why Men Rebel*. Princeton: Princeton University Press.

Gurr, Ted Robert, and Mark Lichbach. 1986. "Forecasting Internal Conflict: A Comparative Evaluation of Empirical Theories." *Comparative Political Studies* 19 (April): 3–38.

Haggard, Stephan. 1990. *Pathways from the Periphery*. Ithaca, N.Y.: Cornell University Press.

Hardy, Melissa A. 1979. "Economic Growth, Distributional Inequality, and Political Conflict in Industrial Societies." *Journal of Political and Military Sociology* 7 (Fall): 209–227.

Hartman, John, and Wey Hsiao. 1988. "Inequality and Violence: Issues of Theory and Measurement in Muller." *American Sociological Review* 53 (October): 794–799.

Hechter, Michael. 1978. "Group Formation and the Cultural Division of Labor." *American Journal of Sociology* 84 (September): 293–318.

Hibbs, Douglas. 1973. *Mass Political Violence: A Cross-National Causal Analysis.* New York: John Wiley and Sons.

Hirschman, Albert O. 1979. "The Turn to Authoritarianism in Latin America and the Search for Its Economic Determinants." Pp. 61–98 in *The New Authoritarianism In Latin America*, David Collier, ed. Princeton: Princeton University Press.

Hoggard, Gary D. 1974. "Differential Source Coverage in Foreign Policy Analysis." Pp. 353–382 in *Comparing Foreign Policies: Theories, Findings, Methods*, J. N. Rosenau, ed. New York: Halsted Press.

Holsti, K. J. 1975. "Underdevelopment and the Gap Theory of International Conflict." *American Political Science Review* 69 (September): 827–839.

Holsti, K. J. 1982. "Restructuring Foreign Policy: A Neglected Phenomenon in Foreign Policy Theory." Pp. 1–20 in *Why Nations Realign*, J. N. Rosenau, ed. London: Allen and Unwin.

Horowitz, Donald L. 1981. "Patterns of Ethnic Separatism." *Comparative Studies in Society and History* 23 (April): 165–195.

Huang, Chi. 1989. "The State and Foreign Investment: The Cases of Taiwan and Singapore." *Comparative Political Studies* 22 (April): 93–121.

Huntington, Samuel. 1968. *Political Order in Changing Societies.* New Haven: Yale University Press.

Ihonvbere, Julius O. 1994. "The Irrelevant State, Ethnicity, and the Quest for Nationhood in Africa." *Ethnic and Racial Studies* 17 (January): 42–60.

Jackman, Robert. 1980. "A Note on the Measurment of Growth Rates in Cross-National Research." *American Journal of Sociology* 86 (November): 604–617.

Jackman, Robert. 1982. "Dependence on Foreign Investment and Economic Growth in the Third World." *World Politics* XXXIV (January): 175–196.

Jackson, Robert H., and Carl G. Rosberg. 1982. "Why Africa's Weak States Persist." *World Politics* XXXV (October): 1–24.

Jackson, Steven, Bruce Russett, Duncan Snidal, and David Sylvan. 1978. "Conflict and Coercion in Dependent States." *Journal of Conflict Resolution* 22 (December): 627–658.

Johnson, Chalmers. 1962. *Peasant Nationalism and Communist Power.* Stanford, Calif.: Stanford University Press.

Johnson, Chalmers. 1966. *Revolutionary Change.* Boston: Little, Brown and Co.

Kaufman, Robert R. 1979. "Industrial Change and Authoritarian Rule In Latin America: A Concrete Review of the Bureaucratic-Authoritarian Model." Pp. 165–253 in *The New Authoritarianism in Latin America*, David Collier, ed. Princeton: Princeton University Press.

Klandermans, Bert. 1984. "Mobilization and Participation: Social-Psychological Explanations of Resource Mobilization Theory." *American Sociological Review* 49 (October): 583–600.

Koo, Hagen. 1987. "The Interplay of State, Social Class, and World System in East Asian Development: The Cases of South Korea and Taiwan." Pp. 165–181 in *The Political Economy of the New Asian Industrialism*, F. C. Deyo, ed. Ithaca, N.Y.: Cornell University Press.

Kornhauser, William. 1959. *The Politics of Mass Society*. New York: Free Press.

Kowalewski, David. 1987. "Asian Strikes Against Transnationals." *Comparative Political Studies* 19 (January): 508–524.

Krasner, Stephen. 1976. "State Power and the Structure of International Trade." *World Politics* 28 (April): 317–347.

Krymkowski, Daniel H., and Raymond L. Hall. 1990. "The African Development Dilemma Revisited: Theoretical and Empirical Explorations." *Ethnic and Racial Studies* 13 (July): 315–344.

Lafeber, Walter. 1984. *Inevitable Revolutions*. New York: W. W. Norton.

LaFever, Ernest. 1962. "Nehru, Nasser, and Nkrumah on Neutralism." Pp. 93–120 in *Neutralism and Nonalignment*, L. W. Martin, ed. New York: Praeger.

Lasswell, Harold. 1936. *Politics: Who Gets What, When, How*. New York: McGraw-Hill.

Leonard, H. Jeffrey. 1980. "Multinational Corporations and Politics in Developing Countries." *World Politics* XXXII (April): 454–483.

Leslie, Winsome J. 1987. *The World Bank and Structural Transformation in Developing Countries: The Case of Zaire*. Boulder, Colo.: Lynne Rienner Publishers.

Lewis-Beck, Michael. 1980. *Applied Regression: An Introduction*. Beverly Hills, Calif.: Sage.

Lichbach, Mark Irving. 1989. "An Evaluation of 'Does Economic Inequality Breed Political Conflict' Studies." *World Politics* XLI (July): 431–470.

Lipsky, Michael. 1968. "Protest as a Political Resource." *American Political Science Review* 62 (December): 1144–1158.

Lipson, Charles. 1985. *Standing Guard: Protecting Foreign Capital in the Nineteenth and Twentieth Centuries*. Berkeley: University of California Press.

Liska, George. 1962. *Nations in Alliance*. Baltimore: Johns Hopkins University Press.

Liska, George. 1968. *Alliances and the Third World*. Baltimore: Johns Hopkins University Press.

Locke, John. 1955. *Of Civil Government, Second Treatise*. Chicago: Henry Regency Co.

London, Bruce, and Thomas D. Robinson. 1989. "The Effect of International Dependence on Income Inequality and Political Violence." *American Sociological Review* 54 (April): 305–308.

London, Bruce, and Bruce A. Williams. 1988. "Multinational Corporate Penetration, Protest, and Basic Needs Provision in Non-Core Nations: A Cross-National Analysis." *Social Forces* 66 (March): 747–773.

Lorenz, Konrad. 1966. *On Aggression*. New York: Harcourt, Brace, and World.

Madison, James. 1961. "Federalist No. 10." Pp. 77–84 in *The Federalist Papers*, Alexander Hamilton, James Madison, and John Jay, eds. New York: Mentor Books.

Magdoff, Harry. 1969. *The Age of Imperialism*. New York: Monthly Review Press.

Magdoff, Harry. 1976. "The Multinational Corporation and Development: A Contradiction?" Pp. 200–222 in *The Multinational Corporation and Social Change*, D. E. Apter and L. W. Goodman, eds. New York: Praeger.

Mahler, Vincent. 1980. *Dependency Approaches to International Political Economy*. New York: Columbia University Press.

Mahler, Vincent. 1981. "Mining, Agriculture, and Manufacturing: The Impact of Foreign Investment on Social Distribution in Third World Countries." *Comparative Political Studies* 14 (October): 267–297.

Mahler, Vincent. 1989. "Income Distribution Within Nations: Problems of Cross-National Comparison." *Comparative Political Studies* 22 (April): 3–32.

Mainwaring, Scott. 1987. "Urban Popular Movements, Identity, and Democratization in Brazil." *Comparative Political Studies* 20 (July): 131–159.

Marshall, Susan E. 1985. "Development, Dependence, and Gender Inequality in the Third World." *International Studies Quarterly* 29 (June): 217–240.

Marx, Karl, and Friedrich Engels. 1959. *Basic Writings on Politics and Philosophy.* Edited by Lewis S. Feuer. Garden City, N.Y.: Anchor Books.

Mason, T. David. 1986. "Land Reform and the Breakdown of Clientalist Politics in El Salvador." *Comparative Political Studies* 18 (January): 487–516.

Mates, Leo. 1972. *Nonalignment: Theory and Current Policy.* Dobbs Ferry, N.Y.: Oceana Publishers.

Midlarsky, Manus. 1982. "Scarcity and Inequality: Prologue to the Onset of Mass Revolution." *Journal of Conflict Resolution* 26 (March): 3–38.

Midlarsky, Manus. 1988. "Rulers and the Ruled: Patterned Inequality and the Onset of Mass Political Violence." *American Political Science Review* 82 (June): 491–510.

Midlarsky, Manus, and Kenneth Roberts. 1985. "Class, State, and Revolution in Central America: Nicargua and El Salvador Compared." *Journal of Conflict Resolution* 29 (June): 163–194.

Migdal, Joel. 1974. *Peasants, Politics, and Revolution.* Princeton: Princeton University Press.

Molotch, Harvey. 1979. "Media and Movements." Pp. 71–93 in *The Dynamics of Social Movements: Resource Mobilization, Social Control, and Tactics*, M. N. Zald and J. D. McCarthy, eds. Cambridge, Mass.: Winthrop Publishers.

Moore, Barrington. 1966. *Social Origins of Dictatorship and Democracy.* Boston: Beacon Press.

Moran, Theodore. 1974. *Multinational Corporations and the Politics of Dependence.* Princeton: Princeton University Press.

Moran, Theodore. 1978. "Multinational Corporations and Dependency: A Dialogue for Dependentistas and non-Dependentistas." *International Organization* 32 (Winter): 79–100.

Muller, Edward. 1985a. "Dependent Economic Development, Aid Dependence on the United States, and Democratic Breakdown in the Third World." *International Studies Quarterly* 29 (December): 445–469.

Muller, Edward. 1985b. "Income Inequality, Regime Repressiveness, and Political Violence." *American Sociological Review* 50 (February): 47–61.

Muller, Edward, and Karl-Dieter Opp. 1986. "Rational Choice and Rebellious Collective Action." *American Political Science Review* 80 (June): 471–488.

Muller, Edward, and Mitchell Seligson. 1987. "Inequality and Insurgency." *American Political Science Review* 81 (June): 425–452.

Muller, Edward, Mitchell Seligson, Hung-der Fu, and Manus Midlarsky. 1989. "Land Inequality and Political Violence." *American Political Science Review* 83 (2): 577–595.

Nie, Norman, C. Hadlai Hull, Jean G. Jenkins, Karin Steinbrenner, and Dale H. Bent. 1975. *Statistical Package for the Social Sciences.* New York: McGraw-Hill.

Nielson, Francois. 1985. "Toward a Theory of Ethnic Solidarity in Modern Societies." *American Sociological Review* 50 (April): 133–149.

Oberschall, Anthony. 1979. "Protracted Conflict." Pp. 45–70 in *The Dynamics of Social Movements: Resource Mobilization, Social Control, and Tactics*, M. N. Zald and J. D. McCarthy, eds. Cambridge, Mass.: Winthrop Publishers.

O'Donnell, Guillermo. 1988. *Bureaucratic Authoritarianism*. Berkeley: University of California Press.

Oliver, Pamela. 1980. "Rewards and Punishments as Selective Incentives for Collective Action: Theoretical Investigations." *American Journal of Sociology* 85 (May): 1356–1375.

Oliver, Pamela. 1984. "If You Don't Do It, Nobody Else Will: Active and Token Contributors to Local Collective Action." *American Sociological Review* 49 (October): 601–610.

Olson, Mancur. 1963. "Rapid Growth as a Destabilizing Force." *Journal of Economic History* 23 (December): 529–552.

Olson, Mancur. 1968. *The Logic of Collective Action*. New York: Schocken Books.

Olson, Mancur. 1982. *The Rise and Decline of Nations*. New Haven: Yale University Press.

Paige, Jeffrey. 1975. *Agrarian Revolution*. New York: Free Press.

Parvin, Manoucher. 1973. "Economic Determinants of Political Unrest: An Econometric Approach." *Journal of Conflict Resolution* 17 (June): 271–296.

Pinelo, Adalberto. 1973. *The Multinational Corporation as a Force in Latin American Politics*. New York: Praeger.

Prosterman, Roy, and Jeffrey Riedinger. 1987. *Land Reform and Democratic Development*. Baltimore: Johns Hopkins University Press.

Przeworski, Adam, and Henry Teune. 1970. *The Logic of Comparative Social Inquiry*. New York: John Wiley and Sons.

Randall, Vicky, and Robin Theobald. 1985. *Political Change and Underdevelopment*. Durham, N.C.: Duke University Press.

Ranis, Gustav. 1976. "The Multinational Corporation as an Instrument of Development." Pp. 96–117 in *The Multinational Corporation and Social Change*, D. E. Apter and L. W. Goodman, eds. New York: Praeger.

Reuber, Grant. 1973. *Private Foreign Investment in Development*. Oxford: Clarendon Press.

Richardson, Neil. 1976. "Political Compliance and U.S. Trade Dominance." *American Political Science Review* 70 (December): 1098–1109.

Richardson, Neil R. 1978. *Foreign Policy and Economic Dependence*. Austin: University of Texas Press.

Richardson, Neil, and Charles W. Kegley, Jr. 1980. "Trade Dependence and Foreign Policy Compliance: A Longitudinal Analysis." *International Studies Quarterly* 24 (June): 191–222.

Robinson, Joan. 1954. *The Economics of Imperfect Competition*. London: MacMillan and Company.

Rogowski, Ronald. 1987. "Political Cleavages and the Changing Exposure to Trade." *American Political Science Review* 81 (December): 1121–1138.

Rogowski, Ronald. 1989. *Commerce and Coalitions: How Trade Affects Domestic Political Alignments*. Princeton: Princeton University Press.

Rothgeb, John M., Jr. 1984a. "The Effects of Foreign Investment on Overall and Sectoral Growth in Third World States." *Journal of Peace Research* 21 (February): 5–16.

Rothgeb, John M., Jr. 1984b. "Investment Penetration in Manufacturing and Extraction and External Public Debt in Third World Sates." *World Development* 12 (November-December): 1063–1076.

Rothgeb, John M., Jr. 1984–85. "The Contribution of Foreign Investment to Growth in Third World States." *Studies in Comparative International Development* XIX (Winter): 3–37.

Rothgeb, John M., Jr. 1986a. "Compensation or Opportunity: The Effects of International Recessions upon Foreign Investment and Growth in Third World States, 1970–1978." *International Studies Quarterly* 30 (June): 123–152.

Rothgeb, John M., Jr. 1986b. "Testing Alternative Conceptions of the Relationship between Direct Foreign Investment and External Debt in Poor Countries." *Comparative Political Studies* 19 (April): 130–176.

Rothgeb, John M., Jr. 1987. "Trojan Horse, Scapegoat, or non-Foreign Entity: Foreign Policy and Investment Penetration in Poor Countries." *Journal of Conflict Resolution* 31 (June): 227–265.

Rothgeb, John M., Jr. 1988. "Direct Foreign Investment in Mining and Manufacturing in Underdeveloped States." *Social Science Journal* 25 (1): 21–43.

Rothgeb, John M., Jr. 1989a. "Direct Foreign Investment, Repression, Reform, and Political Conflict in Third World States." Pp. 105–125 in *Markets, Politics, and Change in the Global Economy*, W. P. Avery and D. P. Rapkin, eds. Boulder, Colo.: Lynne Reinner Publishers.

Rothgeb, John M., Jr. 1989b. *Myths and Realities of Foreign Investment in Poor Countries*. New York: Praeger.

Rothgeb, John M., Jr. 1990a. "Foreign Investment and the Decapitalization of Underdeveloped Host Countries." *Social Science Journal* 27: 457–473.

Rothgeb, John M., Jr. 1990b. "Investment Dependence and Political Conflict in Third World Countries." *Journal of Peace Research* 27 (August): 255–272.

Rothgeb, John M., Jr. 1991. "The Effects of Foreign Investment upon Political Protest and Violence in Underdeveloped Societies." *Western Political Quarterly* 44 (March): 9–38.

Rothgeb, John M., Jr. 1993a. *Defining Power: Influence and Force in the Contemporary International System*. New York: St. Martin's Press.

Rothgeb, John M., Jr. 1993b. "A Regional Analysis of the Relationship between Foreign Investment and Political Conflict in Developing Countries." *Journal of Political and Military Sociology* 21 (Winter): 219–240.

Rothschild, Joseph. 1981. *Ethnopolitics: A Conceptual Framework*. New York: Columbia University Press.

Rothstein, Robert. 1968. *Alliances and Small Powers*. New York: Columbia University Press.

Rothstein, Robert. 1977. *The Weak in the World of the Strong*. New York: Columbia University Press.

Rubin, Barry. 1981. *Paved With Good Intentions: The American Experience and Iran*. New York: Penguin Books.

Rubinson, Richard. 1976. "The World Economy and the Distribution of Income Within States: A Cross-National Study." *American Sociological Review* 41 (August): 638–659.

Rubinson, Richard. 1977. "Dependence, Government Revenue, and Economic Growth, 1955–1970." *Studies in Comparative International Development* XII (Winter): 3–28.

Rummel, Rudolph. 1966. "Dimensions of Conflict Behavior Within Nations, 1946–1959." *Journal of Conflict Resolution* 10 (1): 65–73.

Schatz, Sayre P. 1987. "Assertive Pragmatism and the Multinational Enterprise." Pp. 107–129 in *Postimperialism: International Capitalism in the Late Twentieth Century*, D. G. Becker, J. Frieden, S. P. Schatz, and R. Sklar, eds. Boulder, Colo.: Lynne Rienner Publishers.

Sederberg, Peter C. 1994. *Fires Within: Political Violence and Revolutionary Change.* New York: HarperCollins.

Senghaas, Dieter. 1975. "Multinational Corporations and the Third World." *Journal of Peace Research* 12 (4): 257–274.

Sick, Gary. 1985. *All Fall Down: America's Tragic Encounter with Iran.* New York: Penguin Books.

Sigelman, Lee, and Miles Simpson. 1977. "A Cross-National Test of the Linkage between Economic Inequality and Political Violence." *Journal of Conflict Resolution* 21 (March): 105–128.

Simon, Denis Fred. 1988. "External Incorporation and Internal Reform." Pp. 138–150 in *Contending Approaches to the Political Economy of Taiwan*, E. A. Winckler and S. Greenhalgh, eds. London: M.E. Sharpe Publishers.

Singer, J. David. 1991. "Peace in the Global System: Displacement, Interregnum, or Transformation?" Pp. 56–84 in *The Long Postwar Peace*, C. W. Kegley, Jr., ed. New York: HarperCollins.

Sklar, Richard L. 1975. *Corporate Power in an African State.* Berkeley: University of California Press.

Sklar, Richard L. 1987. "Postimperialism: A Class Analysis of Multinational Corporate Expansion." Pp. 19–40 in *Postimperialism: International Capitalism and Development in the Late Twentieth Century*, D. G. Becker, J. Frieden, S. P. Schatz, and R. Sklar, eds. Boulder, Colo.: Lynne Rienner Publishers.

Skocpol, Theda. 1979. *States and Social Revolutions.* New York: Cambridge University Press.

Skocpol, Theda. 1982. "What Makes Peasants Revolutionary." *Comparative Politics* 14 (April): 351–375.

Snyder, David. 1978. "Collective Violence: A Research Agenda and Some Strategic Considerations." *Journal of Conflict Resolution* 22 (September): 499–534.

Spalding, Hobart. 1977. *Organized Labor in Latin America.* New York: New York University Press.

SPSS. 1983. *SPSSX User's Guide.* New York: McGraw-Hill.

Stohl, Michael. 1980. "The Nexus of Civil and International Conflict." Pp. 297–330 in *Handbook of Political Conflict*, Ted R. Gurr, ed. New York: Free Press.

Sunkel, Osvaldo. 1979. "Big Business and Dependencia." Pp. 216–225 in *Transnational Corporations and World Order*, George Modelski, ed. San Francisco: W. H. Freeman.

Szymanski, Albert. 1981. *The Logic of Imperialism.* New York: Praeger.

Tanter, Raymond. 1966. "Dimensions of Conflict Behavior Within and Between Nations, 1958–1960." *Journal of Conflict Resolution* 10 (1): 41–64.

Tanter, Raymond, and Manus Midlarsky. 1967. "A Theory of Revolution." *Journal of Conflict Resolution* 11 (September): 264–280.

Taylor, Charles, and Michael Hudson. 1972. *World Handbook of Political and Social Indicators II.* New Haven: Yale University Press.

Taylor, Charles, and David Jodice. 1983. *World Handbook of Political and Social Indicators III.* New Haven: Yale University Press.

Tilly, Charles. 1978. *From Mobilization to Revolution*. Reading, Mass.: Addison-Wesley.

Timberlake, Michael, and Kirk R. Williams. 1984. "Dependence, Political Exclusion, and Government Repression: Some Cross-National Evidence." *American Sociological Review* 49 (February): 141–146.

Timberlake, Michael, and Kirk R. Williams. 1987. "Structural Position in the World System, Inequality, and Political Violence." *Journal of Political and Military Sociology* 15 (Spring): 1–15.

Toch, Hans. 1965. *The Social Psychology of Social Movements*. New York: Bobbs-Merrill Co.

Tocqueville, Alexis de. 1971. "How, though the reign of Louis XVI was the most prosperous period of the monarchy, this very prosperity hastened the outbreak of the revolution." Pp. 95–96 in *When Men Revolt and Why*, James C. Davies, ed. New York: Free Press.

Tucker, Robert C. 1970. *The Marxian Revolutionary Idea*. New York: W. W. Norton.

Vengroff, Richard. 1975. "Neo-Colonialism and Policy Outputs in Africa." *Comparative Political Studies* 8 (July): 234–250.

Vernon, Raymond. 1971. *Sovereignty at Bay*. New York: Basic Books.

Vernon, Raymond. 1976. "Multinational Enterprises in Developing Countries: Issues in Dependency and Interdependence." Pp. 40–62 in *The Multinational Corporation and Social Change*, D. E. Apter and L. W. Goodman, eds. New York: Praeger.

Vernon, Raymond. 1977. *Storm over the Multinationals*. Cambridge, Mass.: Harvard University Press.

Wallerstein, Immanuel. 1961. *Africa: The Politics of Independence*. New York: Vintage Books.

Wallerstein, Immanuel. 1974. *The Modern World System*. New York: Academic Press.

Weede, Erich. 1981. "Income Inequality, Average Income, and Domestic Violence." *Journal of Conflict Resolution* 25 (December): 639–654.

Weede, Erich, and Horst Tiefenbach. 1981. "Some Recent Explanations of Income Inequality: An Evaluation and Critique." *International Studies Quarterly* 25 (June): 255–282.

Weiner, Myron. 1960. "The Politics of South Asia." Pp. 153–246 in *The Politics of the Developing Areas*, Gabriel A. Almond and James S. Coleman, eds. Princeton: Princeton University Press.

Wells, L. T., Jr. 1971. "The Multinational Business Enterprise: What Kind of International Organization?" Pp. 97–114 in *Transnational Relations and World Politics*, R. O. Keohane and J. S. Nye, Jr., eds. Cambridge, Mass.: Harvard University Press.

Wiarda, Howard J. 1986–87. "Misreading Latin America—Again." *Foreign Policy* 65 (Winter): 135–153.

Wilcox, Francis. 1962. "The Nonaligned States in the United Nations." Pp. 121–151 in *Neutralism and Nonalignment*, L. W. Martin, ed. New York: Praeger.

Winckler, Edwin A. 1988. "Elite Political Struggle, 1945–1985." Pp. 151–171 in *Contending Approaches to the Political Economy of Taiwan*, E. A. Winckler and S. Greenhalgh, eds. London: M. E. Sharpe.

World Bank. 1976. *World Tables*. Baltimore: Johns Hopkins University Press.

World Bank. 1980. *World Tables*. Baltimore: Johns Hopkins University Press.

World Bank. 1983. *World Tables.* Baltimore: Johns Hopkins University Press.

Wright, Theodore P., Jr. 1991. "Center-Periphery Relations and Ethnic Conflict in Pakistan." *Comparative Politics* 23 (April): 299–312.

Zimmermann, Ekkart. 1980. "Macro-Comparative Research on Political Protest." Pp. 167–237 in *Handbook of Political Conflict*, T. R. Gurr, ed. New York: Free Press.

Zimmermann, Ekkart. 1983. *Political Violence, Crises, and Revolutions: Theories and Research.* Cambridge, Mass.: Schenknan.

INDEX

ABOUT THE AUTHOR

JOHN M. ROTHGEB, JR. is Professor of Political Science at Miami University in Ohio. He is the author of several books, including *Myths and Realities of Foreign Investment in Poor Countries* (Praeger, 1989).

ISBN 0-275-94548-0

9 780275 945480

90000>

EAN

HARDCOVER BAR CODE